A MIRROR
IN MY OWN
BACKSTAGE

Also by José Angel Figueroa

Hypocrisy Held Hostage
Noo Jork
East 110th Street
Unknown Poets from the Full-Time Jungle
Poets of Reason
Children's Language Sandwiches
The Homeland/La Patria
Inner Self

A Mirr⊕r In My ⊕wn Backstage

J⊕sé Angel Figuer⊕a

RED SUGARCANE PRESS
NEW Y⊕RK

A Mirror In My Own Backstage
Copyright © 2013 José Angel Figueroa

All rights reserved. No part of this publication may be reproduced, stored in a retrieval system, or transmitted in any form or by any means, electronic, mechanical, photocopying, recording, or otherwise, without the prior written permission of the publisher.

Published by Red Sugarcane Press, New York
www.redsugarcanepress.com

Publisher, Editor & Book Layout: Iris Morales
Technical Advisor & eBook Designer: Adrien Bibiloni Morales

ISBN:978-0-9884750-0-7
Library of Congress Control Number: 2012952268

Cover Art & Book Design by Juan Sanchez
Cover Font and Logo Design by Walter Velez

Second Edition - 2015
Printed in the United States of America

DEDICATION

To my mother Milagros
and my children
Tamarinda, Guarionex, Taíno,
Chelita and Eddie.

Y a mi querida compañera, Iris

C⊕NTENTS

Reflections of a Scholar
by Edna Acosta-Belén, Ph.D   1
Foreword by Richard Poe   3

A MIRROR IN MY OWN BACKSTAGE

O SHAKESPEARE   17

MURDERED LUGGAGE

MURDERED LUGGAGE   25
MAMA   26
Boricua   27
I Saw Puerto Rico Once   30
Felipa, La Filósofa de Rincón   31
Puertorriqueña   33
"Puerto Rico" Made in Japan   35
Going North   36
Stand-By Airports   39
A Conversation with Coca Cola   42

THE UNSEEN

THE UNSEEN   49
I Used to Think   51
On the word *Minority*   52
The Jelly Bean Policy   54
Side-Swept   55

Ode to Joe Blow Sixpack   56
Man Child   58
EJOOKASHEN   59
Rebel with a Red Dress   60
Endless Time After Time   62

COWBOYNOMICS

COWBOYNOMICS   65
Homemade Smiles   68
Taíno   69
Puerto Ricans for Beginners   70
FOODSTAMP COLONIALISM   73
Pablo Neruda   76
Death Rides A Wild Horse   78
HYPOCRISY HELD HOSTAGE   80
Roasting Amiri Baraka   83
Confessions from the Last Cloud   85

FREEDOM IS MY NATURE

FREEDOM IS MY NATURE   91
Veils & Walls   93
Nakedness   94
The Sniper   95
Womanizer   97
Chulo Puto   99
The Majestic Café   101
Jazzy   102
SATIN LADY BLUES   103
Querida   106

A DAY IN THE LIFE OF A MANIKIN

A DAY IN THE LIFE OF A MANIKIN	111
In Memory of My Talkative Typewriter	114
Different But The Same	115
Song for the Self	116
A Mouth in Lorca's Stomach	118
Saintly Crimes & Faith's Misdemeanor	120
EPITAPH For A DisLifed Metaphor	123
WELCOME TO LIFE	127
The Talking Cats	129
Balladeers & Boozers	131
The Planet of Glass	133
Why Were You Born?	134

NOO JORK: FROM AN ISLAND TO AN INNER CITY   139

Acknowledgments	145
About the Author	147
About the Artist	148
About Red Sugarcane Press	149

REFLECTIONS OF A SCHOLAR

Since his early writings, José Angel Figueroa has carved a distinctive place among the most innovative pioneers of the vibrant Nuyorican poetic movement of the 1970s. This movement first captured the experiences of poverty, racism, and marginality endured by Puerto Ricans in the neglected barrios of the New York metropolis, and rendered their struggles visible through a powerful grassroots performing poetry.

Four decades later, the poems collected in Figueroa's *A Mirror in My Own Backstage* still reflect the author's social and political warrior soul of earlier times, but similarly reveal the creative imagination of a poet with a deliberate "consciousness of Art." For as much as Figueroa's poetry speaks to issues of equality and social justice, it is also an effective aesthetic tool for articulating allegorical visions and ontological musings about our place in a dysfunctional world and the overall human condition.

In Figueroa's poems, there is a confluence of the individualistic and the collective; the poet's own personal memories, experiences, and contemplations are shaped by a keen understanding of the dynamics of history as a continuing clash between the privileged and the dispossessed. While many of Figueroa's poems give a voice and a sense of identity and heritage to a colonized Puerto Rican people, other poems in this volume bare a more introspective, philosophical, and Shakespearean dimension of his writing—the world is a stage where the poet stands as "a mirror in [his] own backstage," striving to visualize and reflect the unseen, make sense of a wounded universe, and breath some harmony into it through the poetic imagination.

What makes Figueroa's poetry so refreshingly unique, is how he branches out from the prescribed social and political messages of the Nuyorican movement and ends up with a more aesthetically and conceptually richer and complex poetry, often tinged with surrealistic tropes or the surprising juxtaposition of images that are simultaneously subversive, healing, and deeply rooted in notions of human freedom and dignity.

A Mirror in My Own Backstage is a collection that gives testament to Figueroa's poetic evolution; it includes some of his most classic poems along with a new crop of innovative work by this accomplished and gifted artist who masters his craft.

Dr. Edna Acosta-Belén is a Distinguished Professor of Latin American, Caribbean, and U.S. Latino Studies and Women Studies, University at Albany, State University of New York. Her publications include *Puerto Ricans in the United States: A Contemporary Portrait* (with Carlos E. Santiago); *The Puerto Rican Woman: Perspectives on Culture, History and Society*; and *The Way It Was and Other Writings by Jesús Colón* (with Virginia Sanchez Korrol).

FOREWORD

Many thousands of years ago, a great king died in Egypt. His name was Intef. The priests prepared a tomb for King Intef, and hired a poet to write his funeral song. The words of this song were inscribed on King Intef's tomb. Throughout the land, harpers sang the song at funeral banquets for the king.

Many were shocked when they heard the song. It was not what they expected. Funeral songs were supposed to be happy and hopeful. They were supposed to talk about the glories of eternal life. A funeral song was supposed to reassure people that the king was alive and well in the next world, feasting and drinking with the gods.

King Intef's funeral song was different. It did not say any of the usual things. Instead, it said that no one knows what lies beyond the grave. It said we can't possibly know, because no one has ever come back to tell us.

Therefore, said the poet, let us eat, drink and be merry. Let us enjoy ourselves while we're here. That's the only happiness we can ever know for sure.

"Rejoice in your heart..." said the poet. "Put myrrh on your head, dress in fine linen, anoint yourself with oils... Lo, none is allowed to take his goods with him... none who departs comes back again!"

We no longer remember the name of that poet. His name has been lost. But four thousand years later, we still remember his poem.

We remember it because it touched people's hearts. Nearly a thousand years after King Intef died, Egyptian scribes were still making copies of that poem. People were still reading it and harpers were still singing it. Moreover, other Egyptian poets began to imitate it. More and more funeral songs began to appear, expressing doubts and fears about what really happens after death. More and more people began to express how they really felt.

We don't know the name of that poet. But, whoever he was, I have a feeling he did not have an easy life.

In ancient Egypt, preparing for the afterlife was big business. A huge funeral industry provided expensive services such as mummifying the dead, festooning corpses with charms and amulets, and providing scrolls of magical spells, all designed to ensure that the dead person made it to heaven. Legions of priests, magicians, morticians, jewelers and tomb-builders got rich from the cult of death.

Now here came an impertinent poet announcing that it was all for nothing, that all that money people were spending on fancy tombs and fancy funerals was wasted. There must have been a lot of rich and powerful people angry at that poet.

But a strange thing happened. Within a few generations after that poem was written, the kings of Egypt stopped building pyramids. They no longer felt comfortable spending that kind of money on tombs. They no longer wanted to make such lavish, public displays of their wealth. The mood of the people had changed. And the pharaohs changed with it.

I like to think that that nameless poet who wrote the Song from King Intef's Tomb had something to do with that change. I like to think that his little song helped the Egyptian people to step back, clear their minds, rethink their priorities and start to see things a little more clearly.

A Conversation with Coca Cola

Nowadays we no longer build pyramids of stone, but we are still building pyramids of the mind. A vast media and entertainment industry devotes trillions of dollars to telling us what we should think, how we should live, and what products we should buy. Not unlike the ancient Egyptians, we have been brainwashed to think that we have no choice. We think that we just have to keep building those pyramids, bigger and bigger all the time, because that's life. But maybe it's not true. Maybe we don't need to build pyramids at all. Maybe if we could just stop and think for a minute, we might see a way out.

That is why we need poets. We need people who will make us stop and think. We need people who can pause, step back from the rat race, and see things in a different way.

When I was a young graduate student at Syracuse University, I read a poem that reset my brain. It helped me see something that was right in front of my eyes, but which I had somehow been brainwashed not to see. The poem was called "A Conversation with Coca Cola."

It was written by José Angel Figueroa, a Puerto Rican poet who grew up in the South Bronx, a world as far removed from my comfortable suburban upbringing as if it were another planet.

I knew nothing about his world and nothing about him. I was not even sure how to pronounce his name. But his words opened my mind.

On the surface, "A Conversation with Coca Cola" seemed like many other writings from Latino and African-American poets of that era, filled with an anger I could not understand.

Figueroa's rage was outside my experience. I did not share it. Whatever he was experiencing had nothing to do with me or my middle-class upbringing in the suburbs of Syracuse, New York.

And then there were all those Spanish words in the poem, words like *bodega, negrito, jíbaro* and *borinqueño*. What did they mean? Even when I looked them up in a Spanish-English dictionary, I still wasn't sure what this man was talking about.

A Common Language

But there was one thing in the poem that I understood perfectly. I understood Coca Cola. I knew exactly what that meant. I knew how Coca Cola tasted. I knew how it tingled in your throat. I knew it was bad for you, because it rotted your teeth.

And I also knew it was powerful. I knew that the Coca Cola Company represented big money and corporate power, on a planetary scale. I knew that Coca Cola could crush me like an ant under its foot, if it wanted to. I knew that, if Coca Cola had existed in ancient times, men would have worshipped it as a god. They would have sacrificed children on the altar of Coca Cola, as they did on the altars of Moloch and Ashtoreth. I knew all these things, but never thought of them much. Then I read Figueroa's poem, and I began to think.

"I speak now / coca cola," the poem began. And with those first words, I was hooked. I understood why a person might decide one day to have an imaginary conversation with Coca Cola.

After all, Coca Cola is everywhere. Wherever you look, there it is. It's in the supermarkets and drugstores and vending machines. It's on TV. It looms over your head on giant billboards. You can't get away from it. And, as I read those words, I understood why a man might stop in his tracks one day, turn his head, look straight into that bright red Coca Cola logo, and decide to talk back to it. I understood that.

This is what Figueroa said in his poem:

> i speak now / coca cola,
> the way a stone is born,
> of your tongue of raw meat
> and teeth like tombstone
>
> you roam east side streets
> where corner lights
> speak spanish every day
> and like picasso
> you want to become
> the soulful dictionary
> of *el barrio*'s feet / don't you

Now, of course, when I read those words, I didn't know anything about Spanish Harlem or *El Barrio*, and I didn't know anything about corner lights speaking Spanish. Up in Syracuse, where I lived, all our corner lights spoke English.

But I understood one thing. I understood that this poet was accusing Coca Cola of invading his space. And we all know what that means. We know what it means when someone invades your space.

Figueroa's poem names many other invaders besides Coca Cola. His poem is filled with all the familiar names of all those mass-market products that were beamed into our brains, as we sat mesmerized before our TV sets. It didn't matter if you were white, black, green, yellow or purple with pink polka-dots. The language of TV advertising made us all one.

In his poem, Figueroa voiced his defiance of Ajax, Clairol, Spic & Span, Alka-Seltzer... even Heinz Ketchup! He accused them all of a genocidal conspiracy to wipe away Puerto Rican culture as efficiently as Spic & Span wipes away dirt from our kitchen floors. And there was something about the way Figueroa said it, something in the rolling thunder of his words, that made me believe him, and made me understand.

The Cry of Blood

In his poem, Figueroa vowed that his people would never give in, that they would never trade their red-hot *picante* sauce for soothing Alka-Seltzer fizz; that Puerto Rican women would never trade "the true meaning of their own existence," as he called it, for the phony blond glamor that comes from a Clairol bottle. He vowed that the Ajax White Knight would never scour clean the memories of Puerto Rican forefathers who had suffered and struggled against oppression.

It was a brave vow, but seemingly a reckless one. Like Don Quixote tilting at windmills, the poet was taking on an adversary that would never quit, never tire, never bleed and never die. This enemy could not be killed, because it had no life or soul. How could a mere poet vanquish such a foe?

How could mere poetry stop the steamroller of global mass marketing and corporate power?

Figueroa searched his heart and brought forth an answer. He found it in the deepest, biological drives of a people determined to survive. He found it in the primal power of Puerto Rican blood, whose flammable mixture of Arawak, African and Spanish genes burst forth in the outcry of artists yearning for their ancient roots. Ultimately, says the poet, what remains is struggle and rage. Justice, he says, "is not a yearly Christmas gift." Those who want justice must fight for it.

When I first read "Conversation with Coca Cola," it was like a message from another galaxy, a subspace transmission from the planet *El Barrio*. But there was something in that message that I could understand. Something that I never forgot.

I still drink Coca Cola now and then, and I still like the taste. But Figueroa did something to my brain. Since reading that poem, I have never been able to look at a bottle of Coke in quite the same way. After all the billions of dollars spent marketing Coca Cola in every corner of the globe, how strange and wondrous that a single poet, with a single poem, could rebrand that product so completely in my imagination that never again could I gaze upon that blood-red insignia of Coca Cola without a ripple of unease tingling up my spine.

The Queen's English

A Mirror in My Own Backstage features new poems and old, love poems and poems of rage, social polemics, slices of immigrant life, and metaphysical visions. It is a worthy retrospective for a distinguished career.

Figueroa has succeeded in breaking out of that tiny, academic ghetto reserved for the Latino or Puerto Rican poet. His verses address all English-speaking peoples with a confident and hard-earned intimacy. Born in Mayaguez, Puerto Rico, Figueroa arrived in New York at age 7, speaking no English. "Coming to school was a daily public execution," writes Figueroa in the autobiographical epilogue that concludes this volume.

Shrewdly, Figueroa chose to "befriend English," and to use its power for the advancement of his people. While his cinnamon skin perpetually marked him as an outsider, Figueroa discovered that, "Reading and writing became my second skin." He delved deeply into the Latino masters, reading Cervantes, Lorca, Neruda, Julia de Burgos, Piri Thomas and many others. But he also immersed himself in the writings of English-speaking sages such as Blake, Hemingway, Mark Twain, Emily Dickinson, Amiri Baraka and William Shakespeare. Figueroa made their language his own. And sometime, during those long hours spent in the Morris High School library in the South Bronx, he made his breakthrough.

The fruits of his labors are obvious. Figueroa has mastered the Queen's English more ably than most native speakers. His verses ring with Shakespearean pentameters and long-line jeremiads rendered in the finest, cascading rhythms of the King James Bible.

When he writes of America today, Figueroa no longer speaks as an observer or outsider. He has staked his claim in American letters, carving for himself and his people an impregnable stronghold from which they can never be driven out.

Puerto Ricans for Beginners

It is possible to read Figueroa's anthology as an epic poem. He attempts to do for the Puerto Rican people what Homer did for the Greeks, Vergil for the Romans, and the prophets of Israel for the Jews. Figueroa creates for his people a national mythology, a story that attempts to explain how they got here, and why the rest of us should be pleased at their arrival. Figueroa's tribal creation tale spills forth from every verse in this anthology. But you will find it set forth most succinctly in a poem called, "Puerto Ricans for Beginners."

The tale begins with a Caribbean Garden of Eden, a place called *La Isla del Encanto*, The Isle of Enchantment. There the Taíno or Boricua people, a branch of the Arawak nation, lived in harmony with the earth. Then Columbus arrived, bringing smallpox, slavery, the Roman Catholic Church, and four hundred years of Spanish domination. The U.S. conquest came next, in 1898. "We did not cross the border; it crossed us," writes Figueroa.

But who exactly are "we"? And who is "us"? Here we get to the nub of the matter. If José Angel Figueroa were to order one of those easy-to-use DNA kits from Ancestry.com, most likely it would show a genetic profile similar to other Puerto Ricans, part Arawak, part African, and part Spaniard. Puerto Ricans are three peoples in one.

When you carry that many lineages in your blood, what does that make you? What is your identity? And where is your loyalty?

Rebranding America, Rebranding Himself

The poet finds no easy or simple answers. In the epilogue, Figueroa admits that, even while continuing to "search for my own roots," he lives in hope, "that America will someday embrace me as part of its own national soul."

Figueroa does not sit passively, waiting for Tío Sam (Uncle Sam) to accept him. Through his poetry, he sets out to rebrand America as audaciously as he rebranded Coca Cola. He envisions the "browning of this great nation," and the emergence of a new, multicultural America, where his mixed blood will no longer mark him as an outcast.

In the transformed America of Figueroa's prophecy, people will understand that "the blend is greater than the ingredients alone," and that our national motto, "E Pluribus Unum – one formed from many" should apply to people of every color.

But this poet understands that "Tío Sam" may not choose to go quietly into the night. He understands that this world we inhabit follows Darwinian rules, in which the strong do not make way for the weak. In considering these realities, Figueroa digs deep, summoning from his imagination visions of apocalypse. And, in his ultimate paroxysm of pain, the poet cries out, not to Coca Cola this time, but to William Shakespeare, the ultimate English-speaking sage and symbol of the Anglo culture.

The Lesson of the Poet

The result is a poem called, "O Shakespeare," which may be Figueroa's masterpiece. It begins with a question:

> O Shakespeare
> I stand before you:
> A mirror in my own backstage
> Wondering what is the lesson of the poet

As Figueroa ponders his purpose on earth, he takes us on an imaginary journey through space and time, from the era when, "Our planet was young, And reason had not yet arisen," through the gropings for consciousness of the earliest cave men, and finally to the present, "Hysterialithic Age," when "The victors and the vanquished roamed freely about," and time itself was "crushed and transfixed" in an "explosion of lifelessness" that "fused the retina of all eyes."

In this nightmare vision, Figueroa contemplates the ultimate Darwinian struggle, in which man's ambition finally renders our planet unlivable, a time when birds fall from a poisoned sky, mushroom clouds give off "neutrons and gamma rays," humanity follows the dinosaur into extinction, and, in the poet's words, "hell awoke from a long hypnotic sleep."

"What kind of scandal/Is this O Shakespeare!" cries the poet. But Shakespeare never answers, and the poet is left to wonder whether introspection might be the only course left, the quest to understand ourselves from the inside out. In his parting words to Shakespeare, Figueroa concludes:

> Perhaps this is
> The lesson of the poet
> As I stand before you
>
> A Mirror
> In My Own
> Backstage

With these words, Figueroa admits that the poet may be little more than an entertainer, a poor player who struts and frets his hour upon the stage, and then is heard no more. Figueroa echoes this humbling realization in another apocalyptic poem, titled, "Confessions from the Last Cloud."

As the poet contemplates a world drained of life by an epidemic of boredom, hypocrisy and entropy, he muses, "Now I'm an innocent by-stander…"

> A tourist of the universe
> The last interpreter of
> History when history itself
> Had been destroyed

In the epilogue, Figueroa speaks as the champion of his people, bravely declaring, "We will not disappear." But he never explains exactly how the Puerto Rican people will manage to avoid disappearing, in that great "browning" of America he envisions, where "one" will be "formed from many" in what will surely be the world's ultimate melting pot.

It is possible that Figueroa has posed a riddle to which he has no answer. And maybe that is why Figueroa turns his thoughts, in the end, to apocalypse and extinction. For he is wise enough to know that, in the end, we will all disappear, no matter what plans we lay.

What really counts, then, in Figueroa's mind, is how we comport ourselves during our brief moment on the stage, and whether we give a pleasing performance or a wretched one. In this present volume, Figueroa has given a most pleasing performance indeed. He is a natural performer, with an actor's sense of drama, and an actor's vanity, keeping one eye always on the audience, and the other eye fixed upon himself, upon his own image, reflected in that mirror which he speaks of, hidden from our sight, in the poet's own backstage.

Richard Poe is a *New York Times*-bestselling author. He has written many non-fiction books on science, history, business and politics, among them *Black Spark, White Fire: Did African Explorers Civilize Ancient Europe?* Poe's latest book is *Perfect Fear: Four Tales of Terror*, his first work of fiction. Poe graduated from Syracuse University with Honors in Creative Writing. He lives in New York City.

A MIRROR IN MY OWN BACKSTAGE

O SHAKESPEARE

O Shakespeare

I stand before you:
A mirror in my own backstage
Wondering what is
The lesson of the Poet.

Is it writing about agility as if
Yesterday or today and tomorrow
Were part of the same climate
As time is measured and digitized
Into little spaces and numbers
That shape human affairs

And whether in agony or drawn
Blood from the skin of words
Revealing to unfold and emerge
To discover how to be born
Naked once again before the
Reincarnation seasons dry out?

Or is the lesson of the Poet
To withdraw when silence
Trembles alone to obey
The unpredictable heart
Taking inventory of old questions
To create the keys for new suspicions

And celebrate the history of life
Whirling about in multiplied-truth
From birth to wounded ages
In blurs and tears that melt
Into songs or decorated madness

Asking: Not what is
The Human Problem
But what mindset or faces
Do we now wear for history?

Once O Shakespeare

Our planet was young
And reason had not yet arisen
Until Nature's lab gave history
Its own blood and Earth surfaced:
Vapors encircled this world
And oceans were born
While all plants and trees
Became individualistic
As Human life first blinked
Was given a fresh view
And its crucible.

We had to quest for what must
Be seen and weave a shroud
To comprehend our caves
So the winds never have
An identity problem.

But now I must reveal
The Hysterialithic Age
And the murder of Earth!

It was inevitable: The victors
And the vanquished roamed
Freely about as if these were
The bruises of some nuclear
Jungle where you could predict
Hit & run realities while
Singing the Victim's Blues.

The question O Shakespeare

Is no longer Why?
But how long before
We call the way we live: WAR!

How long was it before
Teller's Bomb had calculated
Over-killed screams did not
Exist until it happened:

Time was crushed and transfixed
As the sky fell off while
Brilliant light and heat erupted
As fireballs ignited upwards
Expanding the theory of death
A millionth of a second as
An explosion of lifelessness
Fused the retina of all eyes
Shell-shocked and paralyzed
While mushroom clouds
Turned into burnt shit!

All originality became benumbed
And traditions lost teeth
As immortality had its seasons
Fumigated when a pendulum
Of neutrons and gamma rays
Swung into disequilibrium
And raped time while the
Beta and alpha particles
Down-sized into
Ground Zero

Until hell awoke from a long
Hypnotic sleep and equal
Opportunity nightmares
Were totally free!

What kind of scandal
Is this, O Shakespeare

When ancient elephants converge
And go through convulsions
In this Hysterialithic Age

When an axis of cramps
In the atmosphere is changing
This planet into leprosy

When you could look up
And see birds flying
With insects inside them
Eating away their destinies
While assassinated wings
Fall randomly on your toes

When you could also hear
A distant growling incinerating
The forces of the winds
Or feel the whale's integrity
And wisdom of the tortoise
Crashing against the seashores!

Now taste the chemicals
That vomit this air

And tell me, O Shakespeare

Did dinosaurs become extinct
Or did they really leave town?

And must we still quest
For what must be seen anew
To greater comprehend
Our very own caves?

Perhaps this is
The lesson of the Poet
As I stand before you:

A Mirror
In My Own
Backstage.

MURDERED LUGGAGE

MURDERED LUGGAGE

I still remember that first day. We got off with splintered shopping bags and half-panicky the entire family walked out like some rainbow.
I was that skinny dark blue suit, purple shirt and thin black tie, red socks with ring around the heels, always hungry for bubble gum drops.
Tall lanky Carlos stood out the most since his rooster's pompadour made him cocky. And Rubén was the chubby hick who loved reading Roy Rogers & Gene Autry comic books but who never got used to wearing long-sleeve shirts 'cause it always fatigued him.
I remember snow-skinned shy Celia, always hiding her smile ever since one of her teeth ran out on her. And little sister Miriam was the best Puerto Rican thumb-sucker in the airport.
Speaking of sucking-up-to, I did not eat any bubble gum drops on that day: My brother Héctor was the meanest vacuum cleaner from Rincón, and he snagged them from me.
Ah, and *mi Mamá*, Milagros: Have you ever seen such a proud rose with indented cheekbones before? I will always see this miracle as a piece of wind, feeding my mind with the wonders of when and why tree leaves fall in a child's past dream.
I dreamt of that first day: When we reached the baggage terminal, *Mamá* saw our luggage murdered and sprawled all over the cold city floor.
And I still remember this day like some knife stabbing my memory. It was the first time I'd ever seen such a proud and passionate rose, sighing while melting inside snow.

MAMA

You once said you were
a brand new body
whose soft-spoken eyes
opened every morning
before the roosters
translated the weather.

Once your feet
spoke to the floor,
there were no lay-offs;
dishes ripped the smiles,
pots and pans clawed
those sunken fingers,
and clothes that demanded
to be purer than soap
had you blind-stitching
running mad.

The days never seemed
to sing songs of respite
in your name.
None could see your eyes
fallen asleep over the sink
or hear your feet running out
of fuel over the long-heated
hours, nor your heart panting.

No complaints were heard
in your whispers, not even
during the last seconds
of a stolen night when
you shelved yourself
to sleep and still found
the time to smile
in solitude.

Boricua

Boricua: you were
born somewhere
between American Airlines
near San Juan
and Kennedy Airport
near The Bronx
and I have seen
your grim face
listening to bleeding
in the distance
as your mind walks

BACKWARDS
    BACKwards
        backwards

and sees Lincoln Hospital
having a field day
with your mother 'cause
she had labor pains
with a Spanish accent
Remember, *Prieto?*

    Schools wanted
    to cave in your
    Puerto Rican accent
    and because you
    wanted to make it
    you had to pledge
    allegiance left-handed
    when you had lost your soul
    during some English exam

Report cards fed you
with counterfeit dreams
dictionaries carved fear
into your skin and had
a warrant for your accent
because they said you were
always culturally deprived
remember, *Negra*?

    And I often wondered why
    they kept smirking their lips
    when they called you *Perro-Rican*
    instead of Puerto Rican
    but who am I talking
    about, *Negro*?

We're really the same
Youngblood, except I have
seen you drown in multicultural
hangouts in Central Park
where frenetic congas make
unemployed crowds freak out
on people trying to become
a part of one crowd or another.

    And your spirit looks back
    for an island, and

She says:

    I am not all paradise, *Boricua*
    remove your eyes and plant them
    inside my soul; flirt with me
    but glance deeper now.

See infants not yet born crumble
and fire will grow on your lap once
knowing the distance our people
have suffered, my child.

   But never let your mind
   eat silence or wait
   for *mañanas* to dust off
   your anger.

Help her! This island says:

   Help me to silence
   slum poetry by giving
   of self to your people
   so we could eat away all
   those fatty acids making
   it difficult to recognize you
   anymore in airports, stand-by
   airplanes, in the Bronx

Y los callejones de Puerto Rico.

I Saw Puerto Rico Once

    I came from the nest
all birds thought they could find
where the grass spreads
across the common
and the roots of trees
the earth of roads
and the water of rivers
longed my thoughts
to come home again
    I came but the wind
chiseled pointed sounds
down my spine
and the sun blinded
my senses to see no one
who recognized mine
was not a visit
    I came from those hills
mountain forests
and streams of side-grass
in every mind
    but now I fear the nest
may lose its tree
cause the roots below
the grass and the earth
above the soil may
dry and wither or break
the seal which formed
this dream
    and today I wonder
if I will be able to tell all
and find that path again
where the grass walks
across the common
to the front-steps
of my native stream

Felipa, La Filósofa de Rincón
[Que nació a la edad de 83]

FELIPA had life in the blood of her eyes, history in her body. With a cigar half-strangled by her aged fingerprints, she had subdued my eyes and put my words to pulsate with the night. Felipa, *La Filósofa de Rincón* was very tranquil. This bulk of life never took her eyes off my mind.

She never left me alone. I was filled with her voice every sun-baked afternoon beneath a shaded tree of *quenepas*. Her strength raised me like a breeze whose skin was made from the old prophets of our history. *Era el quinqué de la noche*. Her voice was a lantern in the darkness as she held my small hands and walked with my mind toward the blue face of the sky. The sunlight always waited for her. The conversations were warm, gentle yet absorbing. I listened to what went around me with my eyes. Little did I know Felipa was sculpturing my roots.

I could still seep the memories of that last afternoon we spent together when those awesome hills and small valleys paid attention to our footsteps as the spirit of the winds played with the wings of palm trees while the sounds of patience colored the Homeland with solitude. Ah, my soul was spread all over *La Isla* as Felipa blew history in my ears. Listen:

I remember, my child, when proud *jíbaros* woke up the tired mornings and poured their sweat into the hungry soil of the Homeland. These were happier days when our *pueblos* danced to the emotional songs of Spanish guitars, as if inviting *Yuquíyu* to sing our future with the slaves' drumbeat under the taste buds of the sun, while our smiles fertilized any bent or torn days.

Mijo, tripping on love was our only thirst for luxury.

I listened to Felipa but could not imagine the tears drowning in her throat. I was a child insulated from pain and could not comprehend these long-winded words then. Come, return to her memories before mine escape me and feel her voice dive into your ears.

Ours was a life-filled island, my child, where dreams could be found. Until a thick dark cloud invaded the silent faces of long hours when our prayers were tortured by strangers who slept with our future.

Mijo, we had become hostages inside a hurricane with tortuous rain and the unbearable sun of an uprooted earth. Look up and see bullet-holes stab the sky! Our freedom must always be on the guest list of the infinite winds!

Afterwards, I saw the scars suffocated *Abuelita's* prunish body and gazed as if her soul had abandoned this massive skeleton, knowing my own spirit would not be home for many days and nights. We walked back home via a narrow dirt road when the orange clouds blindfolded the sun.

Shhh! *La Isla del Encanto* was mute. Felipa had filled my eyes with philosophy and the history she blew in my ears taught me never to let hope get stuck in my ribs. For hope is harmony. And *La Filósofa de Rincón* once said:

Poeta! You could always kill a hurricane with harmony! With harmony, you could always kill a hurricane.

Felipa, *La Filósofa de Rincón*, was like that.

Puertorriqueña

*Jíbara, Borincana, ¿por qué
te pintas la cara?*

Don't you know you have blended
    the true complexion of the sun
born *Cacique de Flamboyán* to
    caress the wonders of your
breadth, the shape of the thighs
    and curve of your hips made
of *Borinquen's* natural side.

Be like the grass whose floor does
    not need a roof or mirror for
its face with brush-on shadows
    of pearl-like fantasies to give
beauty its name.

    Negra, Africana, why
    bleach your hair?

Don't you know the black silk crop
    & sugar cane African resilience
from which you were born crowned
    your phosphorescence queen
& guided my *Arawak* heels to
    discover the reflections of a
mountainous green world where
    coquí, coquí, coquí define laughter

    & serenity to create the rhythms
        of drums and *maracas* to sing
    & dance when your bewitching voice
        wake up *cemis* who hold hands
with the *canela* hue of my skin.

        Te amo Jíbara, Borincana,
        Negra, Africana!

Whose roots flirt with *Borinquen's*
    abysmal beauty & gave these eyes
my birth & compassion its place
    knowing it will never need
a different roof, nor your face,
    Puertorriqueña, will never need
another name.

"Puerto Rico" Made In Japan

Somewhere from the mountains
of Caguas streams looking flat
flow in every tide painful reflections
down the river and to my home.

Tourists push each other with
starving cameras to show Boston
they had seen celestial winterless
wonders like San Juan natives
dressed in cream vanilla sunshine
suits or Carmen Mirandas eating
Uncle Ben's minute rice.

And sometimes smiling
Puerto Rican doormen.

Yet they return home via American
skies with gorged cameras and
juggled images of our Homeland.

But someday the winds will
misbehave and the rough edges
of the sea will thicken as the
Puerto Rican doormen
continue smiling

When *La Isla del Encanto*
pushes them off the echoes
of hotel civilizations.

Going North

We came
& now lean on
tall buildings

Speaking *dos* languages
at the *mismo* time that
choke your mind knowing
we're 3000 miles apart

& in the coming years
during the hours of early
morning front stoops

I've seen brothers & sisters
enjoying the fake sun
Warner Bros. bought
for its new movie

Mornings when we
zigzagged through
hip streets flying dreams
across an ocean too deep
to understand our souls

Days when we bathed
our stomachs by injecting
dreams in our veins about
Wall Street suntan lotion
& electrical hopes

& then it happens

Somehow
we keep going back
to romantic nostalgia
landing on cultural
plenas y *pasteles*

Only to find that
McDonalds is living in
Mi Viejo San Juan

& coming back
to model cities under
the Hudson River

& going back
when the Latin dances
got very expensive

& coming back
when Eddie Palmieri
made a new album

& going back
when mumbling legs
could not swallow
blind cold winters

& coming back
when you high-jacked
your mind when you
couldn't speak *español*
for one curable hour

& going back
when you realized
you've been inside grey
walls ever since you mixed

Voy pa' Noo Jork
con sugarcane *ron*

Or:

Coming   Coming   Back

Back   Back   Going

Going   Going   Coming

Until you run out of
Tic Tac Toe conversations

Stand–By Airports
to Dilys Laing

She took the train far away
from herself when her face
was terrorized by the years
dripping by on the window sill.
She walked faster, stumbling
over her mind until arriving
at a bus.

   She thought:

I need change and wheels
always move revolutions. I
must surpass old ideal dreams
and must get somewhere
before the future falls blind
on me.

   Her face said: Breakout!
   Escape! Don't look back!

This time she landed in a plane
and flew passed the incognito
blues. While a flight attendant
with mesmerizing eyes, stuck
his tongue in her ear. And for
an encore, kissed her bare feet
and ate her sacred forest.

> Love should have changed me
> into a woman, she thought.

The clouds dressed in tuxedos
turned into jazzic musicians who
played sidemen with the shade
and sunlight of the moon as she
fell asleep and left her nakedness
dancing with stolen memories.

> The flight attendant returned:
> We have landed, Ms.

Opening her eyes, allowing the
warm air to enter her nostrils,
she sprang to her feet, still
aroused, ran down the cat-walk
and touched the ground.

> A crowd came to embrace her.
> Their laughter attacked her
> worn body:

Father, mother, siblings,
hubby, children, lovers
the whiff of some friends
and avid tormentors had
evaporated her presence.

> They move as fast as I do,
> she thought.

And seconds later, she wanted
to cast off and climb the clouds
again.

    The airplane vanished, Ms!

She faced the crowd, screaming:
I've love all of you but the one
whose habits of violins & violence
I have long abandoned!

    They laughed without mercy.
    Don't you recall? You had
    kidnapped her and made a
    U-turn! You look disembodied.

But don't worry: You'll always be
Welcome Home.

A Conversation with Coca Cola

i speak now/coca cola
    the way a stone is born
of your tongue of raw meat
    and teeth like tombstone

you roam east side streets
    where corner lights
speak spanish everyday
    and like picasso
you want to become
    the soulful dictionary
of *el barrio's* feet/don't you

don't you know
    that bodegas feed *negritos*
and *picante* makes the food feel good
    so your alka-seltzer communions
won't be necessary to digest
    that yellow *latino* grease
which makes rice *pegao*
    the only confirmation
and constitution of our land

don't you know
    that new york *jíbaros*
Will never give in to dixie peach
    and plus white toothpaste philosophy
and that *jíbaritas* will never carry
    their hopes in high heels
to become deaf and dumb to the true
    meaning of their own existence
in exchange for miss clairol's
    push-down spray and dead traditions
of does she or doesn't she
    miss subway realities

i speak now/coca cola
    the way a stone is born
for the plaster that came crawling down
    from the tired blemished ceiling
from above that loses its vision
    when night invades
the voiceless will of day/woke me up

    and told me the only life
which made sense anymore are those graves
    that can't speak english
and which are kept from crying
    like pigeons sleeping in the rain

and told me/coca cola
    the only sense which made life anymore
are those restless streets
    that get ulcers everyday/knowing
borinqueños are held in dying tension
    ever since ajax nixon
had sent that white knight
    to clean spik & span's mind
from knowing that the red stains
    of the sweat and pain
of his brown and black flesh
    was nothing but the ketch-up
mr. heinz left behind
    before he made you
the king of *latino's* brow

and told me/coca cola
    that *latino* souls wake up
like swollen dreams
    in the middle of the night
ever since con edison raised the rent
    and the landlords executed the hot water
that was to come back from retirement
    before the month's rent

made itself welcomed to molested mail boxes
    who couldn't speak spanish
or spell *latino* names correctly
    unless he's called
tito and maria or chico and mr. spik
    the one with the welfare tribe upstairs

i speak now/coca cola
    knowing you had suffocated
the only air left from
    my flowery-carpeted room
and that your roaming thru *latino* streets
    had caused perverted corridors
street alleys and tar-smelling roofs
    to become the final playground
and cemetery where *el barrio*
    gets babies born with Death Buttons
pinned to their Life Day nipples
    while parked cars have funeral processions
for those who get hit by brute winds
    and cold drunken nights
every morning-day-night

but now/coca cola
    i speak the way blood vessels break
and how saliva can turn to fire
    for the aging paint of my cracked walls
revealed my sleepless eyes the truth:
    that *latinos* have for too long
been succumbed to that religious diarrhea
    of walter cronkite liberals
who wrote the yellow pages of liberty
    and nursery rhyme jack and jill
went up the hill jive
    to handcuff *jibaro's* mind

but now i can see
    like the corner lights
that speak spanish everyday
    and realize why snoopy
was always nodding
    and took his ass to the moon

for he knew/coca cola
    that unemployment agencies
which were now opening on sundays
    would never stop tropical sons
and african daughters
    from crying out:
mami! mami! tengo hambre!
    i'm hungry/bellyaching
every morning to the next
    from an overdose of suffering

for he knew/coca cola
    why ray barretto kept slapping
his mad conga while crying out:
    de donde vengo/ de donde vengo
where do i come from?
    when you made *latinos* suffer
from lack of sun and homemade
    mama/papa skin love
and rice and beans which made them
    men and women and baptized
their morning naturalness

ah! but his message touched
    the ear drums of my mind
and told me/coca cola
    que la justicia/that justice
is not a yearly christmas gift

THE UNSEEN

THE UNSEEN

*Life's but a walking shadow
and thereby hangs a tale.*
- William Shakespeare

they are quite often stared at
but hardly seen crawling
further into night near
your home, school or office

yet they who are so many do
not hide inside their clothes
or conceal themselves in sleep

for these are the unseen
mushroom ranks of faceless
platoons of dehydrated souls
with dry burnt lips
and downcast sterile eyes

who stumble endlessly like
beshadowed bundles of
curled laundry thrown out
of the commonplace

to scramble nowhere and rot
in idleness like desperate
flower heads planted in the dark

where the horror is a mellow
rhythm for abandoned hearts
bitten by stray dogs

as they commit their hunger
to the crimes of scavengers
by hustling pity with hands
roped around their faces

to smuggle the past in a huge
luggage of memories full with
cigarette butts and ashes

so they could bribe insatiable
death and pawn old age
for the silly little things

while fading off before
the naked eye

I Used to Think

Adapted from a Jules Feiffer cartoon

My name is Being.

I used to think
I was Poor.

Then they told me
I wasn't poor.

I was Needy.

They told me
It was self-defeating to
think of myself as needy.

I was Deprived.

Then they told me
deprived was a bad image.

I was Under-privileged.

Then they told me
under-privileged was overused.

I was Disadvantaged.

I still don't possess
an education

But I do have
a great vocabulary.

On The Word *Minority*

The Word turns
people of color invisible
it splits the homeland
and sucks the air from
the bloodstream until
it overshadows the solar
plexus cultivated to be

The Program

The Word *Minority*
is damage control
a controlled substance
the godchild of war
against poverty.

It is a gifted child playing
slum wizard over
Olympian nightmares
in doghouse schools

The Word is a bum rap

An ego alien projection
a code for bio-underclass
to repair the subjugated
at-risk from becoming the
Lazarus of sub-minimum
wages against the brute
force of life-coping skills
sweating in the palms
of society

The Word *Minority*
is a caste system with a
cast call without an audition
when by nature the blend is
greater than the ingredients

Alone.

The Jelly Bean Policy

The man who ironed
shirts and ties
for twenty years
tried to claim
disability pay for his
state of boredom

He was given
an application to fill
in triplicate
but instead ate it

The civil servant
fell blind to all this
asking: can I help you
write a suicide note
instead?

Everyone laughed
but the laughter had
its own impressions

And he felt like
a hostage doll
given jelly beans
to play with

SIDE-SWEPT

You Are
Invited To
Pink Slip It

& Follow
The Load
Out There

You May
Bark. Beg. Bitch.
Appeal Or Resign

But You
Must Exit

If You Dare
Freak Out:
Be Warned

We Will Talk
About You
During Dinner

And If
Our Beloved
Children Laugh

Blame It
On The
Remote Control

Ode to Joe Blow SixPack

Joe Blow was just another SixPack
who shared a torn memory with its
own graveyard across the outskirts
of gridlock city.

Great hobos, jobless saints and
honorable drunks knew him as
a two-fisted wannabe boxer,
shuffling from brawl to brew with
an educated jab to undercut his
opponent but his own shadow
won each and every round.

Relentless, all Joe Blow SixPack
craved for was one last shot to die
of fame and prayed the Almighty
would throw the dice in his favor.

All he got was deuce! Snake Eyes!

Between rounds, Joe Blow worked
as an unemployment claims teller
for the state of alien certifications.

Never a household name, he hung
by his fingernails on a tightrope of
hope when he was downsized and
forced to face the same fate as the
revolving Have-Nots frowned upon
by the olive-colored pencil-pushers
before signing their asses on
the line marked **X**.

This morning, Joe Blow SixPack
went from nobody to head-liner
when he came to the state office
dressed as a boxer then marked
his **X** and blew his brains out to
simply remove himself from the
occupational nature of things.

Man Child

They met; she was The Play
and he The Act.
She became a mother;
he did not.

The child grew up as
a miscarriage, a stranger
who was never allowed
to ask difficult questions
but often heard impromptu
reasons for the simple ones.

Today was the last time
he was going home to prison,
got fed up with the one-night
affairs and nerve-twisting
insults during the bathroom
wars, biting his sleep.

He just had to break from
this savage hope and went
into oblivion when mom took
an epic coffee break with an
overdose of TV sunburn
and soap operas to escape
her diet of miracle pills.

Born-in-exile, he roamed
the spontaneous moment,
slept with the misbegotten,
woke up just as invisible

And named himself Man Child.

EJOOKASHEN

it's boldly cold out there
in the front steps of
ejookashen where *nolij*
is a dead eyebrow
with a real genius
trapped inside

when there's no today
about tomorrow for
children willing to trade
the world for automatic cash

before the bell rings
and the homework season
becomes guerrilla
warfare again

while teachers who were
once honored by lost
traditions & hungry minds
are fed to angry tribes of
the night as they ride
shotgun for toilet-trained
bureaucrats hunting down illiteracy
when the scapegoating rap
is in high gear for
standardized minds

yet it takes only one
to be so many
who do so much
to get a hold
on the essentials of life
and feel meaningful

Rebel with a Red Dress
for Iris Morales

When all my moments
are taken I'm baking
social justice bread
for humanity.

If ambivalent
you don't know
what you stand for.

I'm looking for revolution.
Don't bring a problem
without a solution.
(I'm sorry doesn't
mean action).

When the route of your
soul forms a revolution,
you didn't get loving,
only criticism.

I rebelled and refused to be
the martyred daughter;
to go home and return to
the madness of throwing
failure in your face.

There's nothing to feel
guilty about; acting out
of guilt gets you old.

I am a genuine
accidental actress
with many roles:

An activist who stood up
against the powers
that crushed free-will
and the voiceless.

An educator who taught
children to think out of the
box and dance with gravity
to sleep with the sky
and create their own
language sandwiches.

An attorney who wore
fire-engine red lipstick
to kill asinine misogynists
with godly pajamas in
court and Wall Street.

A producer who devoted
her life to the struggles
for social justice,
racial and gender equality.

"Our challenge is to examine
not only who we were," she says,
"but who we're becoming and
to inspire our communities to
engage in human liberation."

Endless Time After Time
to George C. Stoney

It is such a groove when you
Create the time to live in a world
We believe in where the fellowship
Of social intelligence maintain
Loyal understandings balanced with
Life-long dreams born to be free
To unite the sun of all
And the world of many
To own the future together
Endless time after time

The common heart is not of self
But in building community
Where humanity is deep-rooted
In a treasure of goodwill wrapped
Around inspirational waters
As an act to liberate old knowledge
When freedom demands
Fresh wisdom to question
The making of power or
Privilege of consumption over-
Burdening natural rights to peace
Endless time after time

While those intrinsic values,
Love, Friendship, Home &
A sacred moment of grace: that
Heartbeat in the rhythms of us
Searching, finding, having
And yet in a collaborative spirit,
Let go to become a decisive whole
When we discover a bond so divine
As unity within a place for all
We are undeniably inseparable
Endless time after time

COWBOYNOMICS

COWBOYNOMICS
for Louis Reyes Rivera

Go home, America

But you may never know exactly where
and home is now a foreign affair

An alliance with hideous tyrants
and oligarchic dictators
holding peace ransom by treachery
with purple hearts that seduce
the filthy rich marching with the saints
to resurrect the profiteers by brutally
impoverishing the noble poor
who worship boldfaced liberation!

As these pot-bellied autocrats
ambush the assassinated dead by
ripping off the tongues of prayers of
widowed mothers and stolen wives
who sleepwalk to sniff or kiss
those demised then embrace
to heal their own wounds

When there could be no question
the doves that pray by day
turn into bats at night to play
with vultures in early morning
and rape virginity before it is born
so they could all withstand
the wild stench of freedom!

Come home, America

Shift winds or hit the road
and get off the next exit

But perhaps you may not be
that aware home is now
a foreign affair

A flea-market where mice
and rat patrols turn amok
like scattered shadows
under a drunken moon

To plea-bargain with the flies
and insects for chopped off
genitals or mutilated breasts
and the rampaged eyes torn out
of children's faces when
diehard cynics trade aspirations
with right-wing maggots

So they could all scrounge
the Heartland and dance
passionately the tango delta
with ravaged nuns before
sucking Death from its anus!

Return home, America
Remain to patrol
your own heart

But you may never know
exactly where when home
is now a foreign affair

An outward-bound backyard broker
set adrift from dusk to dawn between
plantain trees and bamboo skies
passed all these roadblocks and
side-roads of genocide to mount
its flag on uprooted winds with
rattlesnake eyes to bewitch
the drumbeat of war dogs

Who get unscrupulously drunk
on amnesia before asking
with prick diplomacy for the
neurotic fascist daughter's hand

So they could all bankroll
the pomp and pride of the elite
in the name of National Security!

Stay home, America

Come and shift winds
or hit the road and
get off the next exit:

Return to yourself
and remain to patrol
your own heart

But you may never know
exactly where nor perhaps
be that aware home is now
a foreign affair

Where American is no longer
spoken anymore!

Homemade Smiles

"My Son," she said:

The bombless skies
applaud your face
innocent voice
winded cheeks and
homemade smiles

WAR is no longer
lovesick for a palace
of honor and rice
peoples' wounds

Your father no longer
salutes the morning news

Our next door neighbors
no longer need to see
an American flag
smiling behind you

And as I look into
a deep hole
of tomorrows

I see harrowing hell
with fleshless bones
of Vietnam spilling
your blood and
voicing you back

After so many nights
wild-eyed and
brimming with tears
"Tell me, my Son:

What good news, could
you - a grave - bring?"

Taíno

it was strange

when my two year-old
shot and killed a bus
with his mid-finger

but then things made
more sense

when my 8th month son
dragged himself
up the sofa

took the NEWS and
slowly destroyed
the Vietnam War

it died gently at first
until he deep-felt
and clawed his fingers

in its history

and as i saw everything
crumble into blood
on the floor

i saw no casualties
just a dead war
and many tomorrows

Puerto Ricans for Beginners

U came from that creation once nature
Left in isolation when the *Arawak*
Nation was later exterminated when
Spain was persuaded the New World
Would soon forget it

400 hundred years U were disgraced
By this god-fearing conquering race
Until 1898 befriended your fate
With more oppression & subtle hate
The only glory that U ate

When an American president moved
In as your new resident since U
Were in some confusion about this
Spanish-Gringo revolution when
U became a nominee for his Manifest
Destiny to be enslaved as a colony

Yet there were times U rebelled
When your lifestyle was instant hell
Where you had not human right
& for this you had to fight

Once you U knew this racist fool
Made U his Bootstrap tool
& a joke to emigration
When your political status
Was a total question

But in this good & plenty *sitio*
U don't cry but *íay bendito!*
For these mail-order dreams
When it all seemed U were
Treated as a lower-class diet
& for this U had to riot
When in 1917 America had
A new idea & invented a game
Called bingo making U a Free-
Associated second-class gringo

When things were terrific Tío Sam
Sent U to the South Pacific
Where U fought the Japanese
Which he then won with ease
& all U learned was *Plitz*

In this gateway mecca U prayed
For fame *La Gran Manzana* USA
When at home U were left astray
& cause U were greatly distressed
The U.S. Navy took over *Vieques*

While U worked in *mucho* factories
Where dying slowly was unsatisfactory
Knowing U could go nowhere else
To make U *mucho* more with less
When all U got were complications
Or six feet under from this mess

So blame *Vieques* for the seeds of
WW II It's the real Pearl Harbor
America never knew

Until Tío Sam led U to this other war
Where U fought against Germany
When genocide was the enemy

Until 1948 when U fell bait to this
Elected traitor who told the
Sugarcane workers the problem
Was the economy but who instead
Sold-out our cultural history
For a commonwealth status
As a mistress with a mystery

When the hope & trauma was
A struggle for a national identity
Minus the Bread, Land & Liberty!

Now ready to face the Red Fear
So Tío Sam sent U to fight Korea
& for an encore the Vietnam War
& a grab-bag of countries denuded
Of rain forests or farmlands
Called *Nada*! Behold Cuba!
Santo Domingo! Grenada!

Think Palestine! Iraq! Afghanistan!
Nicaragua! Desert Storm!
Oil & world power!

Then listen now with a receptive ear
When all U hear are the silent
Tío Sam trained to be nonviolent

& it is why U must
Ultimately decide to
Puerto Ricanize America
Before it's too late:

Let organic freedom be
Borinquen's fate.

FOODSTAMP COLONIALISM
A Don Ricardo E. Alegria

In the plazas and *pueblos* of Puerto Rico
during the light of dawn
the skies grow pink and purple
and *La Isla del Encanto*
is left with bohemian gypsies
searching for shattered exiled dreams
En Mi Viejo San Juan.

Where I first met *El Zorro,*
the priest of the underdog
as he whisked by like an illusive fox
escaping the Colossus of the North
who bestowed upon his people
a commonwealth of self-doubt
to lament lost dignity.

"I was born," said *El Zorro,* "to be
a self-made mad man
wearing the shadows of death
where the Star of the Caribbean
wavers blindly under the realm
of the conquered and kept
when trusted hands once came
with the cross of heaven and
crucified our language of earth
so we may experience democracy
on the installment plan of
foodstamp colonialism."

El Zorro blew my mind
but I stood quiet.

"Well," said *El Zorro*, "I too will
announce my own silence
for I cannot continue my story
unless I'm dancing for the dollar."

And once given his dollar,
El Zorro danced.

"No!" he shouted, "I'm not a sideshow
nor act of Congress gone berserk!"

"I'm not some *jíbaro* or neorican
dressed in Coca Cola clothes
loving salsa music weekends
while trapped in a tourist crowd
rapping disco bebop Spanglish
in top jive-five overtones.

So please take note
why between-it-all
I'm this remote.

I have seen the wealth of outsiders
taking a sip of our hospitality
while purring the air with
the godspell of false kisses
paralyzing my neighbors with
hands glued to their knees
like overtaxed refugees
whose sugar cane dreams
turn foul when the ghosts
of factories closed down
heaven forever!

When I know of so many
who crave for work,
not the humiliation of
federal crumbs or psychic wages
with wholesale prayers so we
could reawaken as a ghost-town
for rented souls with
a theater of military games
and room-service politics
leaving the Homeland
absorbed in its own silence."

¡*Qué coñocarajo!* I thought.

"Well," said *El Zorro*, "if this
is the so-called shinning Star
of the Caribbean, then democracy
is a thief and I'm the unofficial
saint of *El Viejo San Juan!*"

Pablo Neruda

I heard from Pablo Neruda
we must continue reawakening
the Unused Dreams of statues;
then he was dead.

And after the earth ate his flesh,
all I could think of were poems
portable poets would someday
write about Neruda's verses
leaving his body and falling
into the saliva of his soulmate,
friends, and enemies.

I had to do something of his
death. I don't know; something.
Scream feelings inside him, or
perhaps swallow the ruthless
smiles those soldiers killed him
with during that invasion.

I don't know, open every word
he wrote, tie the syllables on
a page and intertwine them to
hang fascism by its horrid throat.

WHAT?

I heard Neruda answer me.
Poeta: thrive on my hangovers.
Let your mind wander in the secrets
of forests, but never blame the
nights for the roots of solitude.

Open yourself to the gifts
performed by this earth;
teach our revolutions never
to mourn blindfolded freedom.

Poets must puff new life
into words and nourish the
consciousness of Art.

They must go to bed with life
and jump over death without
ever hurting their toes;

And wake up to the songs
of poetical bartenders whose
hangovers create far-out poetry.

Believe me, Poeta: it's the only
way statues could ever confess

Any Unused Dreams.

Death Rides A Wild Horse

Death came from twilight at a moment's notice
And ate a tornado for breakfast to bebop with
The midnight moon. It was in the Evening News
Bragging about out-staging the god-forsaken
Weather.

The anchor asked *Death*: If destiny is in the hands,
Where's fate? It replied, "Fate is where silence
Stops the cradle of life before you face me."

Death described itself as a roguish son of a bitch
Who felt quite at home in the frenetic streets
Of chaos. And who is out to eat the vultures.

These included despicable child-molesters,
Malicious misogynists, royal pricks, homophobic
Fart-heads, holy tyrants, hate-mongers, rabid
Rapists, demonic sadists, incorrigible politicos,
Corporate scum and global capitalists of
Human conspicuous consumption.

Hollywood moguls, talk-show superstars
And the Vatican vamped each other's heart
For *Death*'s *Exclusives*.

They tried to entice him with forgiveness rehab.
Age-defying cosmetics. An air-conditioned
Chocolate coffin. *Pan de Muerto*. Free parking
Meters for the dead. An Irish Wake Cake from
A slice of the moon. A culinary recipe for the
After-Life with a Quantum Leap to starve famine
And make warfare absolute. A lively history of
Mortal fears and obsessions. Wall Street dirty
Money. Sex on a wild horse with a virgin.
Hawaiian orgasms. Red-hot lips with a heart
Born of geography to fillet the soul.
Pure fresh air.

Instead, *Death* warmed over with the
Loving eyes of a woman called *Art*.

HYPOCRISY HELD HOSTAGE

What mockery! These chronicles
Of the puppet masters who
Indulge in frolicsome spectacles
To campaign for applauds
And dim the contradictions with
Lip-fornicating promises
Mixed with intellectual piss

While parading in fundraising
Dinners to impersonate the truth
By dissipating the problems
With an abundance of incumbent
Small talk to forecast dangerous
Nonsense with snookering faces
Immune to shock as this new
Cold War dies in the eyes
Of mad sheep!

These puppet masters are gross
National products, appearing
Before closed doors like shrieking
Nuggets of neurotic crabs and
Stockpiling scavengers who change
With the drift as if politics was
Another Broadway Show switching
From donkeys to elephants into
Brooding messiahs & superstars
By swarming from land, air or sea
To audition with grin or contempt
And bite off the kneecaps without
Ever wrinkling your clothes!

And in the mornings, they have
Breakfast with our asses as we
Twitch, itch, and scratch in silence
While analyzing the kind of circus
We live in: Be it true or false
Or none of the above.

Meantime, all else is normal.
Computers hunger for more
Human habits. The poor still eat
Grunt stuck on dinner plates
To balance their budgets.
The winds entrapped in the
Illusions of clocks leave behind
Acid rain with strange ashes

While rocks still dream of walking
Outside of themselves: Perhaps
Feigning death but not fate.

Yet out of all reason, lost & found
Philosophers wander like off-
Springs of Cassandra, musing why
The history of misery remains
Illogical as these puppet masters
Lust for necromancy to rehearse
War on pinball machines and
Eclipse the living by equalizing
The dead: And checkmate.

But nor could we survive these
Ballistic games by moving out
Of the government to play frisbee
While these cockeyed scoundrels,
Jackals, sovereigns and bears
Manage camouflaged deceptions
Like Judas!

Once these tacit charlatans delude
Each other, we're all pawns of this
Bidding war: Aligned or not. Native
Or alien. Naïve or obscurant.

The bet is not on The Outcome.
Nor if the dead yield higher
Dreams of voodoo shit-balls
Or cheese-made eulogies
When even in great disguise
Death reverses itself.

It has no immigrants, only obese
Disciples who gravitate when
The winds fall to bet on the impact
Of this pending storm.

Until all that's left when the
Squirming germs and delirium
Declines is A Shocking Editorial
Written in noble blood with
Unsalted oil:

And the rare distinction between
Human tears and the howling of
Animals heat-frozen in hellish horror
When hypocrisy is held hostage.

What mockery!

But do not bitch or mourn:

Think
And become
Your own
Revolution.

Roasting Amiri Baraka

How do you roast
a raging raisin
with blazing eyes
burning the blank page
until you redefine the
integrity of *Black Fire*

How do you roast
an avenging prophet
who could only trust
the kiss of sacred leaves
from an Ancient Tree
to restore oceans of
ancestral bones erased
from our own history

How do you roast
a rapid fire sage
with an Ebonics-plus
ballistics attitude glued
to his bloodstream like a
clenched fist while every
shadow sings the blues
when the sun rises

While America is all cheese in the
vile global village of virtual TV
waging warfare-for-profit when
bread & butter justice turned
into purified disillusion

How do you roast
a spitfire warrior
who knew America was
truly the Lone Ranger

& that Poetry is
not hypothetical
but an act of war

How do you roast
such a raging raisin

You don't

Instead you honor this
Black Prometheus of New Ark

Who rose up like a talking drum
with an aura of love & stole fire
from the uncool & boring

To combat the apocalyptic
American terror of greed, hunger,
fear, hatred, sexism & white
supremacy raining colonial clouds
of degradation upon a race
under siege when there's
no rhythm in the sky

To enshrined the blues of wild
forbidden sidewalks & shed light
on the obscurity of this madness
Until you redefine the
integrity of *Black Fire*

Confessions from the Last Cloud
for Victor Fragoso

In 2012
The Lone Ranger was executed
Simply because
He was a Republican

This year the leftover
Population forgot all about
Tonto cause natives were
Non Personas per se
For this same reason
Gurus took over the news
To survive oblivious hang-ups

Hang-ups were discovered
To be hereditary

And in 2012
Hell was tired
Of living underground
And the last headlines read:

WORLD WAR III WANTED!
(To Have Intercourse
With Dr. Strangelove!)

This year farted
Days rain-clotted
Nights went completely mad
Dreams had nightmares

Rocks awoke from a long sleep
Mornings grew shattered
Anarchy was out to lunch
The crossroads of unintentional
Circumstances were lonely
Mick Jagger and Peewee Herman
Became human again

Mary no longer pretended
She was a virgin
God became speechless
Marijuana was proven innocent

The CIA died of sore eyes
And politicians could no
Longer barricade their nights
With police lines

For in 2012
The president of the United
States declared war
On his own toilet paper!

This year false prophets
Were convicted
For indulging in fraud

Elephants became extinct
Cartoons lost their struggle
For human civil rights

The morgue had no vacancies
Immortality was last seen
Bleeding two inches
Above a grave

And the last echoes were
Heard gasping over
Deserted mountains
Undocumented shadows
Until Death finally changed
Its name to DRY PRUNES

Now I'm an innocent by-stander
An unemployed cloud
Destined to die of boredom
By working for a lifeless planet

Yet I will be what I've always been:

A tourist of the universe
The last interpreter of
History when history itself
Had been destroyed

An unemployed cloud - Yes!

But also a visionary
Tripping on the gentle
Whispers of love

And who will eventually be
The first citizen of the moon
In the 21st century

FREEDOM IS MY NATURE

FREEDOM IS MY NATURE

I had my first boyfriend at 15, was married by 16 and had 5 children by 22. My cash-poor parents forced this regular guy on me. Some years later, I left him. I met your father, *Don Pepe*. He was a gypsy rogue who was always after my cupcakes, zigzagging and dancing like a crab in broad daylight until he managed to find his way to my front door.

He was also a gambler who loved to tell delicious jokes until early morning, laugh all night, and after a few stiff drinks, get into an occasional brawl, just for an appetizer. I had my own household by then until your father shoved his feet into my door. I was petrified but reserved. I swear I did not know whether to laugh or die!

Once in, that handsome charlatan had declared his manifesto. He had a gift for words, but was just as demanding. His fancy shoes were glued to my floor. No one could dare ask him to leave. Not my god-parents, neighbors, or muted suitors. Not even the devil could show its face! That lover came to visit for just a few minutes and stayed for 35 years!

He was perfectly shameless, and wouldn't know what to do, if he had it anyway. *!Era un atrevido!* Daring! Of course, I fought him all the way, a little afraid, but I loved that beast. He was insatiable!

Those first days were good and bad with some bad mixed with good. Our first home was built before an oceanfront. It was made of wood, straw, zinc and branches with a floor composed of sand. Well, the sea grew fierce and stormed our house, although it did not take it away. I was forced to return home, alone, until a new one could be built.

My parents never welcomed your father.

We were all *campesinos* then. We lived, worked, loved, struggled, laughed, and survived. I used to sew handkerchiefs, make gloves, brooms, and straw hats to sell on the road and plazas. Times were, you could make a dress for 25 cents a yard! Men wore *Pra-Pra* straw hats and tip-toed like God's gift to fainting women. The women wore anything resembling the heavenly virgins.

La Musica Brava was the survival of the wretched poor. It helped to kill the terrible times when there was no work, no rice. *Nada*. Somehow, we never allowed one of our own to die of hunger. Until we had to escape the homeland to exist and scatter our children like sandwiches to our god-parents, aunts, or distant cousins. They were all small-town saints; *siempre bregando con la bendición*.

Life was that way, *Mijo*. We were forced to let our tears vegetate before the harvest and work in the fields of foreigners who gave us empty shacks. Proud *jíbaros* would travel ahead from field to field, town to town, when the lucky ones were called. The wives followed.

I woke up earlier than any rooster I could remember, put on my overalls, a brown shirt, straw hat, and mount a truck when it was my turn. I planted beans, grew gardenias, picked black peppers, squash, cabbage-heads, peas and carrots, everything! My hands were made of sugar cane and salt!

!Era una ganapán! Un café macho! I was a headstrong, wage-earning woman who worked much harder than any man, including *Don Pepe*. I just sometimes wonder if the soil of America even knows my name.

But it doesn't matter. The less you complain, the younger you remain. Yesterday is now, and the future is around the corner. Tomorrow will never wait, unless you get there first.

Yet we survived, my son. And I am still side by side with your father, *Don* Pepe, as I am, with myself.

Freedom is my nature.

Veils & Walls

he wanted
her veil off

to see
the features

she wanted
his walls out

to feel
the space

Nakedness

I'm not in fear of being loved
But in terror of not recalling
I've loved during an impractical
Moment when we crossed paths
With nebulous emotions
Raining desires and doubt

And to catch your glances I left
My nakedness hidden in the
Midnight blues of a wind born
From a mermaid's first kiss

I'm not petrified I've gambled
With passion and left my poetry
In your bedroom to be bedeviled
And wake up like Snoopy with
A split personality hangover

I'm not a recycled lover
Behind some beguiling smile
Whose silence once killed the
Laughter of left-over happiness

Am not that death which drains
Or kills the lover nor that
Stranger you slept with for a
Lifetime in a free-style script

Am not the right or worst of
Times but am just as imperfect
As nature's own like a mountain
Reaching upwards to kiss
The sky as a labor of love

The Sniper

Watching her move made
my tongue park on her.

My eyes landed between
her legs, pensively,
smuggling these lips
while my mind slowly
parachuted over her
climate.

Embracing her moist lips,
plucking them, nibbling;
we couldn't hold this
Explosion, too late!

Colored with passion,
our eyes kept tasting
each other; sweat burnt
the sphere, groans
began bursting as dazed
eyebrows ripped open
the spitfire of night.

Sinking her head deeply
into the pillow, she
put her arms around my
shoulders, glanced at
my hungry mind and
felt my drenched hair

as she glided back and
pushed my mid-finger
against her trembling,
loving lower lip.

My tongue was filled
with her.

She was erupting, her eyes
mumbling for air in earthly
splendor, silk, and silence.

"*Coño, Mami,* you're a sniper!"

And her smile touched me
Goodnight, hoping for a rerun.

Womanizer

ONCE upon a tale unknown
before the noiseless foot
in the mirror of time was
still solitude's sand pile:

Was a mystical island
where only women resided
as the earth's neighbor
loyal solely to the seas.

During the Indian summers
when silence was serene,
these ever-womanly would
dance before this vibrant
pink sun sliding down the
ocean; embracing a pale
blue moon at midnight.

Deep, wondrous and as
powerful, the freehearted
she-lions would snub the
known cynical posturing of
the crabs; these devilfish
acting with emotional cool
the innate heartlessness
in the history of Man.

When suddenly mermaids
had surfaced, holding sea
horses in their arms who
then transformed into males
upon touching virgin sand.

Before them was the naked
horror: the wisdom of the
penis; known to conquer if
not possess to consume and
spit out with masked emotions,
bedrock hearts of passion.

But Earth Mother stood
forth well-heeled, and she
commanded Man be warned!

Never mess with apples
or turn trusted kisses into
bitter fruit. Nor use fire
to act cold.

Turn off the machine in
you, the terror of returning
love; for when fire sleeps
inside fire, it burns hot
and cold in heat and ice.

No need to spice such
freedom, turning love old.

Mindless the right to be:
Honor at home.

Chulo Puto
Honoring Gladys Ricart

Don't ask me why he shot her. It was like a wrong dream. I could only recall her smile was still intact. Now she's gone.

¡Coñocarajo! She's dead. But she wasn't not too long ago before the devil came and the economics of love turned into vengeance.

I know. I was the wedding photographer who shot her before he did, except I clicked and he snapped. We first met in a botanical garden. She was a bride's maid who strayed from the photo shoot and wandered into The Tree of Life gift shop, when she crossed eyes with *Don Chevere*.

Era una Amorosa. A love rose who walked with the rhythms of the moon and spoke with her smile. Her lips electrified him. He went totally *plátanos*. Breathless. She thought he was a wow. *Un chulo puto.* He rarely disagreed with himself. *¡Diablo!* She's dead.

Amorosa could not imagine *Chulo Puto* was allergic to monogamy. Nor could she foresee theirs was an all-or-nothing dead-end when his deaf and blind spots nailed him to her demise.

But this was no crime of passion. It was pure unadulterated murder! The tyranny of PMS: Problematic Male Syndrome.

Somewhere between a whisper, a kiss, and a sigh, she felt a paralyzing odor of deception. She could not imagine herself as a side-dish for some pussy-surfing *politico* who demanded she play the great understudy, *La Otra*.

Don Chevere needed her to be anonymous, ignorant or kitchen-tested and just as beautiful before the silence became a storm. His kisses were the suffering wisdom of doubt.

But *Amorosa* chose to be a one-man woman, not *La Gran Puta* in some water-cooler scandal. When he could no longer see inside her, *Chulo Puto* was lost.

He smelled there was another lover when Precious smiled behind his back. Someone stole his poetry. Jealousy pimped him off until *Chulo Puto* deep-froze and ziplocked his rage. He made love like a hiccup. *Amorosa* never forgave him.

Rebuffed, he began counting the hairs on his chest to see if she had killed any. He blamed her for his sperm retention headaches and was in self-denial when it was his pit-bull cologne.

Yet something was deadly wrong. The minotaur with his genitalia wrapped around the shoulder, could not take it anymore. *Chulo Puto* had a hoof to grind with undying devotion.

It took just one more smile before her vows went from pandemonium to penumbra. In daring to dream wearing white, *Amorosa* saw red. Chulo Puto shot her three times and the love rose died like an expert.

No, please don't ask me why *Amorosa's* smile was still intact after *Chulo Puto* popped her.

Bad endings are wrong dreams.

The Majestic Cafe

    Open at every hour these sweet
but sour pick-a-uppers
when it's raining in your blood
like a downpour of boiling pain
and the truth becomes the fault
unless new headaches refrain
    Acting subtle and lazy to be
afar or weary-free dancing
with the muses triumphant
but just as crazy which ever way
the winds may be
    And the tone of these dreamers
flying high and far too long
on the rosebuds of old songs
never knowing what went wrong
as time drags on and dawn responds
to the tune of the blues
    Thinking of an empty life
with dangling heads in midair
feeling deep or wayside-out
rough and full of strife
when the spirit's torn by doubt
laughing scared with despair
    Trying to justify these roguish lies
and put a demise to separate times
closing the gap between the skies
in illusions fit or cut-to-size
    And the tone of these dreamers
flying high and far too long
on the rosebuds of old songs
never knowing what went wrong
as time drags on and dawn responds
to the tune of the blues

Jazzy

Left my name in many
    Books of matches
Gave & blew some light
    Kept an eyesore on
The score & all the
    Scratches between
Restless days &
    Sleepless nights

So come on Honey
    And let's go home
We don't need to
    Sleep all alone

All I want is us to rhyme
    And place our minds
On harmony
    Just you and I
Becoming we
    So please don't stray
From this melody

Cause I've been in love
    With love before
And even more didn't
    Know what for

Cause I've seen my
    Shadow and heard
These lies I've been
    So multiplied

So come on Honey
    And let's go home
We don't need to
    Sleep all alone

SATIN LADY BLUES

The Life and Times of Billie Holiday

She was a good high yellow woman
with almond-shaped eyes
born to sing how the nights
sometimes grown old and then untold
like an accolade quite blasé
of beautifully ugly problems
whispering mornings may never come
like a sabotage of the mind anchored
to confusion in a bottomless stream
overflowing with elusive times
and bittersweet melancholy
with life as a one-night stand
shipped and sealed for despair
reaching nowhere to be treated
half-home or lacking words and far
less time without any everything

"And Momma may have Poppa may have"

But bless the child who becomes his own
beyond that blink and sigh blemished
with tears while singing to survive
and masquerade the streetwise
waving pride to zigzag through these
swaggering changes when pushed or
haunted by shattered moments
feeling discarded and diffused
like a slow saxophone solo fading off
into obscurity as the piano player
mellows down this war that's never
quite the same the morning after
when a child becomes a holiday for pain

Yet in voice and skin Lady Day traveled
the whole night once ever more
to subside or blend in and sing
of these self-concerns to comfort
the trifled spirit in a subdued rage
weighing more than her legend to mend
each wound as the darkness descended
by approaching the microphone with
resilience showing how it really feels
being a maid and mistress to fiasco
between the new-man cures and cold turkey
or stray dogs and desperate revivals

Blaring the spirituals with
heart-spinning blues to put new wings
on expectations and turn anticipation
into gold with dignity while
holding on to a piece of time
and stuff shadows into silk dreams
with maybe this or maybe that
perhaps today and why not

Living her songs without regrets
to cross over and burn this pain
out of loneliness while improvising
a tonality for chilled laughter between
the Honky-Tonk or rap-talking times in
Tin Pan Alley with top hats and tails
and away from the sun-splashing
sidewalks or hot bisquits to kill
the shock from bad whiskey and put on
a new ensemble of self-respect
to sing with pleasure why sadness
puts a tag on you: and clean out
the sky of its strange fruits

Asking who really knows and if you care
of how southern poplar trees bleed
and agony embodies the air
of subtle prayers that rot in gloom
and dangling bodies cannot compare
how far-in can grief close these eyes
and scream updated with the times
when death brags and never changes
and these processions are combined
with minds now broken into danger
when in the thick of all-in-all
first-rate hatred makes a brusque call
of more half-tones and deeper shadows
and exclusively from across the tracks
where corn whiskey succumbs to sorrows
while crocodiles mingle in rough dance halls
riffin' this outrage before tomorrow's
when spinning the wrong way on poplar trees
and far past backwards with this breeze

But Billie Holiday always kept bouncing
right on back to confront all these
absurdities and understand what rhythms
such ways and times entrapped before
winding down and becoming a prisoner
of her own great myth: Remembering
never to forget love could ever be over
when you can wake up singing

With white gardenias on your hair

Querida

It's two in the morning where
    the night grows into its own
planet of deep inner cities
    bringing you to mind and
that last dance we invented
    of two lovers gone awol
while breaking night
    dancing so wind-minded
you could relax a cobra.

There we were: You and I
    a mixture of bones and raw
sounds feeling the distance
    in hip suave nuances
while foot-stepping beyond
    proximity shaping hellishly
tongue-kissing mantras
    to change the climate of
self-location in non-words and
    revelations searching for the
gut in hidden philosophy or
    counting raindrops without
false moons to out-grow the
    sharp edges of predatory reason.

And I: With flowers flipping from
    my fingers pledged every smile
to the solar system memorizing
    extra hard to forget the thick
lines and walk with your mind

without flapping my thighs
like vicious piranhas biting deep
    through the layers of your skin
when the goodnights changed
    into hard shit hello.

And you: Self-exiled in sanctuary
    and cloned in silence blinking
half-speed to my impulses to keep
    your libido on its toes while
tearing my history completely apart
    to deduct if the performance
on my face was dangerous.

And I: Not really knowing if you
    were smiling or simply showing
me your teeth as you stood there
    just as cocksure with brisk
questions to declare your own
    song without the bedroom wine
or Freudian slip turning words
    into bouquets: Wanting to loved
not chosen, collected or sedated.

There we were: You and I
    breaking night in authentic
poetics making up forgotten songs
    with that last dance flying from
our heels at two in the morning
    to dislodge these grappling
conflicts and discover the distance
    between your voice and mine.

And I do love, Querida:
    What else can I say?

A DAY IN THE LIFE OF A MANIKIN

A DAY IN THE LIFE OF A MANIKIN

I was born during the grasp
Of uncut hours standing there
Like None Other watching reality
With a short neck while
Retrickulating Death as time
Consumed everything.

Too many questions drowned me:
Was I an undeclared birthday
Or did I die in advance?

I had to know. To discover if destiny
Once lived on my hips. If I had
Ever mimed spontaneous walk.
Run in cellophane castles.
Felt my breathing slowly emptied
In the mornings and danced
With the sunrise.
If I had ever witnessed days fade
Into night. Seen nights turn apolitical.
Blink before kissing nostalgia.
If I had ever soul-searched near
The glimpse of a bridge to fathom
Why an ocean never had a vertebra
And face the moon for solace.

I had to find out. At first I tried to
Catch the metaphors between
The revolving doors but English
Was not simple anymore.

I began listening to the darkness
Swim inside me. Grabbed its shape.
Borrowed the personality of midnight
And let the rhythms of moonlight
Expectations brush my hair to catch
Silence wearing desire under its
Nude faces and learned to laugh
And cry to shed a human tear
When you struggled with one hand
And loved with the other.

Yet I felt strange. Pushed. Bent.
But could not move or sleep
With my own eyes as anonymous
Faces kept passing by while
Neon lights guided the traffic.

I had to know. Was I born
Or manufactured? Were my natural
Odors stolen? Or was I the cruel
Joke of a gambling philosopher's
Seductive imagination?

I had to find out. To get wind if
Some mathematical equation
Could confirm if the humility of
Being was truly a godsend
And to unearth if my flight in
This world was canceled.

But I have no more time to taste
The neurotic winds of fear or
To ponder why I was not born
A naked tree instead who once
Craved for the language of air
And the wisdom of water.

Now I live in broad daylight and
Inhale the mainstream to publish
My memories in midair while I
Subscribe myself to tomorrow
As it plays its significance on me
Like an exile from the illusions
Of time to feel the cry of yesterday.

I guess: Until I could declare myself
Better next time.

In Memory of My Talkative Typewriter

THE STORY
goes that my nights
are really long ropes
of tied-up voices:

an ocean of dreams
spilling &
saying so
much & yet
knitted to
silence

knowing my
memory not
so well, I
search for
my Talkative
Typewriter
in the dark
& like some

breathless
informer
flood and
push these
countless
thoughts
out of me
before the
words get
tangled with
rust and
a blank-blue
s t a r e
leisurely
befriends me.

Different But The Same

I want to sing under lights
dim low and flow
from the horns of forlorn
of faces that fade
during every hour feeling
time deadbeat and sour

Once compassion the
moonlight harden
a garden of promises
that come and go
but no one knows
why it must be so

Let's stop this hopeless
yearning when I'm
burning to feel her fire
and forward these
dreams it seems when
passion becomes desire

She was constant in all
her charms but as
elusive within my arms

I was persuaded and
pursued when she
evaded then subdued

I was elated and besides
she was as salty
as streetwise

I was passion and she
the flame cause we
were different
but the same

Song For The Self

Need to keep on walking
And feel my eyes
Being everywhere
Don't really care
For long conversations

I am my destination

What has been done
Has been said
But I refuse to forget
To remember now
I am set for me
Engulfed by the winds
Mellowed with its moods
Have no time to brood

I sing a casual song
Short and simple
I interweave and love
The past was a silly game

A truth mixed with expectations
Still no one's to blame
These contradictions fade
Once they are tamed

Need to keep on walking
Being everywhere
Can't look back anymore
What for?

The questions don't work
Tired of redundant answers
When why is why
Because is because

Then was a name once
Remembered when enough
Was done and said
There was no more
But instead

Hey! Stay away!
Don't display yourself!

I am not an adjunct
Or supplementary
It is all elementary:

Where I'm from you're not
And where we're at
Is another story
Can't look back anymore
And feel sorry

What for?

I don't mind singing
With myself
And I need to keep on
Walking
To keep on walking

With myself.

A Mouth In Lorca's Stomach

Singer of gypsy roads
who carved the waters
of dark blind doors
through the middle of
an early dead afternoon

And came to a full-time city
where life is no dream
but a collective insomnia
heading for the waterfalls
where people dance
the Dance of Death

For the living
who scream their feet
upon the rage of graves
that once spoke
through dawn's mouth
of fiery grass

Like Eliot and Lorca
I ask: what
should I do now?

Should I like many
bleed my fingernails
and open that door from under
the sight of bushels of air
and steal the gold teeth
from those who no longer drown
from an engine of tears?

Or must I, like Lorca
cultivate grass
in the mouth of Death
when the moon shuts
the linens of silence
before a statue of night!

If so, then Lorca's sword
has already touched the moon
long before my eyes
got stung by skyscrapers
when the final gulp
of this gypsy's peasant wind
allowed my voice to pass
through the whip of strange sleep!

Saintly Crimes & Faith's Misdemeanor

woke up
non-aware
struggling

memories
neither here
nor there

shadowboxing
against the paralysis
of analysis

swallowed
by the past
forgetting
the future

healing

yet these memories
return like virgin
whores raping the soul

while facing
the mirrors
of the *I* in *We*

-living life
trapped
in confusion
tasting pain
in the warfare
of others

-rewinding
the tears
of deliberation
plea-bargaining
with the politics
of torn memories

what does it mean
forgiving one's
memories?

-pay less taxation
for doomed hope
before shifting into
the reconciliation blues
or scorn vengeance
to become the architect
of renewed equilibrium

what does it mean
forgiving without
crucified denial to
forget the horror
implanted in silence

-does it mean
laughing anew
without condemned
complicity hiding
the truth of a child's
murdered smile
while longing for the
innocence of peace

what does forgetting
a little mean so that
the *I* in *We* is reborn?

-does it mute the
sexual assault or
repair the ugliness
in multiplied violence
and where could
the beatings blotted
out retire to push
these crimes deep
beyond the nagging
wounds

the answer is not in
our excellent credit
history or in some
over-the-counter
philosophy needing
not original sin or
the wounds of primal
fear while needing
less a cross to bear
and the burden of
isolated recollections!

it is in waking up with
the grace of fresh wind
healing while walking
on rice paper
in the here and now

becoming
homeward bound

EPITAPH For A DisLifed Metaphor
for my brother Héctor

I just don't know how carte blanche
your birth was or how many novels
you lived through before your guilt
had its second wind.

Perhaps you lived through
one too many novels.

Perhaps we could interrupt the archery
of half-moons and take another pause
to exchange tears with a child's whisper
and catch the dawn when it rehearses
narcissus farewells or wasted songs
and teach loneliness to rest with dignity
as we submerge past weightless afternoons
while the world slips in a rebirth of
maybes without emergency exits.

Then watch as these thoughts freeze
on their faces who turned numb
after you had smacked your brain
from its axis!

Should I now preprogram dream control
and erase any arguments to make sure
the nights do not drip on you anymore?

Should I put your anxieties in a museum
or donate your cheeks to some nonprofit
ouch monopoly for strangers just as exiled
from the seasons!

Perhaps if you dislife yourself again
while you're dead the reverse will happen
and we'll learn just how faithless suicide
could be and together stand up and wave
our hands from balconies reserved
for heartbeats on the rebound.

Maybe I could brainstorm with these
ad-hoc mourners gathered tonight and
show them how to eat insomnia sandwiches
while telephone operators lobby in Washington
for extra sensory perceptions.

Maybe I could teach them how to escape
this grief and give crucifixus to random
subway passengers in memory of retired
grave-diggers who substitute sleep for
frozen nights while we continue to taste
dreams in our mouths.

And in the morning after witness how
we could still fix our faces according to
the weather or whatever other etcetera
command shapeless astronomies when we
lose our eyes to unforeseen constellations.

Maybe we could swallow these fantasies
and like gypsies dance around your skull
to let your mind know your wounds were
getting too crowded.

Perhaps then we could take you home
and show how the heart is still capable of
inhabiting an entire population and slowly
shape your voice with the fire in the mouth
of a woman.

Perhaps then we could still party and use
your coffin for biological purpose
and for an encore train these flowers
to navigate its fragrance and camouflage
insanity when it rains.

Maybe after all this we could sit around
and watch if these grave-diggers take this
very lightly and throw their shovels away
without being afraid Death remains
on the prowl like unpainted furniture
nodding in variations of:

Oh Yeah. Sure. Okay.

But knowing perhaps there aren't
anymore maybes and that you and I
could no longer turn the mornings
full blast like two monks on marijuana
and kung-fu into perfect smiles.

Or Slap Five and make obscene phone
calls to jive in national slang and plagiarize
torn pieces of laughter to change the Bronx
into an anthem or just hang out and simply
become an avenue of our very own.

Then perhaps I should wait until you've
been buried and like Lorca or Neruda
follow your darkness behind these leftover
memories and hide myself in the distance
of your silence.

And if I discover some flame near you
pulsating new birth should I freeze this
fire in opium and bring it back as an
abandoned child wrapped tightly from
the rumors of wind.

If so I extend this poem, my Brother.

Para Mamá

And for poets searching eternity
for greater translations when the rain
stops asking just as carte blanche
for a surplus of the hereafter

For its own destination.

WELCOME TO LIFE

After a cocktail head from
the Songs of Clockwork Zoos
I walked through my old
childhood school when I saw
a youngblood stealing himself
from me. Afraid, he snapped
back and sat in a fetish position
staring through the dark.

His eyes long dead and dried,
he moved snail-like, saying
nada,while wrestling to raise
his raincold body from the urine
stench of an O.D. grave.

Diablo! Diablo! he screamed,
as if a hundred congas took
over his velocity and plugged
his juices.

I shifted words and blurred,
"Take it light, my Brother."

And he screamed at the walls,
knuckle-bones bleeding, biting
his veins as he pushed me into
silence.

"Help me! " He cried.

I looked at his head nodding like
Coltrane rhythms trying to touch
the ground like a hammer killing
a nail in midair, wishing I was that
alley to comprehend the darkness
he was in.

"Remove me from this coffin!"
He pleaded.
"Give death a refund!
Welcome me back to life!

I am your Brother."

The Talking Cats
for Tamarinda

Walls walls walls
seem to hang
from their faces
silence silence silence
buried deep inside

And besides the times
are for rapping
in top jive-five

If not to depussify
before you die
like some dumb fly
with the brains of
a messiah and the
soul of a mosquito

For the night is to
rumble with passion
and love like a real
outlaw eating your own
heart to stay alive

And shake off frozen
souls with bad vibes
dancing so electrified

Like cheeze doodles
bebopping wild on
jungle streets rarely
missing a single beat

Keeping up
getting down

Cause reality' is a war
and nobody's taking it
anymore

Cause the groove
is to get-it-on without
dying

Acting cool
and I'm not lying

Balladeers & Boozers

Here! Here! My Patron Hearts
Here's to bartenders and
Barmaids who met them all

The charmers and alarmers
The barfly beachcomers
These whiskey johnnies
And tear-jerkers with
Tiger milk brandy
And drunken companions
Acting like puffballs
Dandies and dandelions

Here's to bold pretenders who
Know-it-all from nonentity
To the Dead Sea Scrolls

When in the end it won't
Matter if your mind
Begins to brag or stagger

As long as you don't
Get lost in the no exit
Cruel history of night

And take a moment to ponder
All that hope and wonder
Could ever bring from
Old fashion romantics
And slow nostalgic songs
Without any semantics
Of lost lovers gone wrong

When you whiff and gulp
Against depression
To riff and laugh unbroken
With a mocking moon's grin
To overshadow the unspoken!

Well here's to the truth
And its very few friends
For life must never
Become a mockery
Behind a crooked smile.

Here's to poetry!

Here's to life!

Here's to loyalty
Against dishonor
And strife!

The Planet of Glass

It was a planet made of glass, homeless art, mixed nuts, plastics & mirrors; a place where time lost its aura & nostalgia was outlawed for indulging in fraud when some humanoids stood trial for stealing wisdom from long forgotten enchanting books.

This was an atrocious crime The System could not forgive.

For this, all humanoids were poisoned with doubt to taste repenting desires and give way of all flesh before succumbing to those frantic dust of

metallic lungs called Man.

What was their crime? It was not combining the eyes with the mind to meet the imagination or seek warmth from naked ambitions to be seduced by the human spirit.

Rather, it was a daring and foolish attempt to be child-like and kiss a bankrupt smile in a museum of wonder so they could learn to laugh anew and perhaps feel intimacy before asking life for its meaning.

Why Were You Born?

I do not write; I am written.
The translator appears.
A great silence implodes.
Words explode. Imagery
Raptures me.

I come. Before I came.

Nada. Not a syllable.
Couldn't spell for beans.
Befriended rice
And stayed alive.
Danced until the musicians
Staggered. My poetry
Was mambo delux.

I do not write; poetry
Writes me.

A walk between two corners
Of a sidewalk changed
My life. A misguided soul
Whispered aloud near me,
He was approaching suicide.

I was on my way parallel
To his passing. He was
Anonymous to my senses.
His eyes begged for relief.
I blinked and listened
With understanding.

I stood closer. Observed,
Absorbed and waited.
Walked slower until we
Were side to side. I asked:
Why were you born?

He was nonplus and just
As plugged. His breath
Could faint a fire hydrant.
I was beside myself.

Passersby burned their
Hips expressing it.

A man once full of desire
Came to his last page:
A play thing for a
Dog's pig ear.

I do not write poetry.

Am not a lifesaver.
Nor could teach you how
To swim in mud.

I walked into his eyes.
Let my own fears drown
In his blood. Questioned
His non persona. Climbed
His cross. Descended
Before the clouds enraged.

I stopped walking.

Reality was just ahead of
The curve. I reminded him
I knew him less than most
But will always remember
We said hello and farewell
All-in-all at once.

He kept ahead and came
To an abrupt end a split
Second before crossing.

I was his last few words:
Cappuccino, or brewsky?
He laughed. I died.
We got drunk on life.

Next thing we knew
We danced under the rain
Like two children never
To grow old ever again.

NOO JORK:
FROM AN ISLAND
TO AN INNER CITY

Noo Jork: From an Island to an Inner City

I still remember that first day. It was 1952 and Mama was proud to announce we had finally arrived at our new island called The Bronx.

"Your first In-glish lesson," said Mama, "is to learn how to say *hamburger* to make sure you do not starve when asked what you want to eat. Forget about yellow rice and beans with avocados. Think American. Our language and cultural spirit will not be welcomed nor accepted. Meanwhile, eat peanut butter and jelly sandwiches until you learn more difficult words." We learned a new word each day before school started.

"But Mama," I asked, 'what if we forget to say *hamburger?* What then?"

After smacking some sense into me, she replied, "Say *French fries!* And if you still forget your second lesson, say *ketchup!*"

My brothers and sisters learned English by reading the eyes of strangers while remaining humble. This determined if they were friendly neighbors or cold-blooded assassins who smiled before crucifying you for daring to embrace the American Dream. But the message was clear: America was private property. Hands off! We had to grow up fast – and in perfect English.

As a ten-year old with silent eyes, timid yet pensive, I was seen as a foreigner and called *Perro-Rican* while laughed at by kids who invented bubble-gum racism. They were highly offended by my beautiful, deep accent, cinnamon skin and very lively tropical clothes. It was a time of great prosperity yet greater fear for this new wave of newcomers. Perhaps if my face and color was depicted in Norman Rockwell's paintings of Americana, I would not have been a victim of educational oppression.

Instead, I was the funny-talker they loved to hate. Learning to speak *In-glish* while acting American became an undeclared tug-of-war. If I chose not to think and act like Dick and Jane, I was punished for speaking Spanish and sentenced to clean the blackboard. Jose, can you see? The U.S. invaded Puerto Rico in 1898 and branded me *Foreigner!* It was pure murder.

Coming to school was a daily public execution with poison pouring from their eyes. Some actually aimed, cocked the mid-finger and shot dead-center through my Spanish heart. But my dignity was bullet-proof. Shouts of *Mira! Mira!* were hard-nosed attempts to deface my self-esteem. It was a blatant conspiracy to make me feel insignificant while treated like some nonentity called *Other*. In short, I was an ego-alien projection.

"But why?" asked this ten-year old. Why? Didn't they realize that I, like them, was *E Pluribus Unum* – one formed from many? Why must English be used to dominate my thinking rather than to cultivate my mind and creative impulse? Why not English-plus! I felt as if all the *I.Q.* and reading tests were an outrageous attempt to invade my Boricua identity, if not to color me invisible. When this did not work, I was straight-jacketed into some dull, characterless room that was disguised as a remedial slaughter-house for the "slow learner" who was also "culturally deprived." Naturally, I was the minority who was intellectually disadvantaged. Which came first – the label or the stigma?

I learned to speak American with an accent. I was less the newcomer than a prisoner of the New York City Board of Education who was pulled back, pushed aside, and railroaded into classes where learning was some dead-end dream.

I felt English was some gigantic nuisance or adversary on a mission to sabotage my Puerto Rican essence, blasting me with the Who, What, Where, When, Why and How!

I was entangled in a web of assimilation and acculturation. It left a lasting impression on me. Frankly, the kind of education I received I would never give to a rock. When I wasn't making colorful pot-holders in home economics, I was drawing perfectly beautiful square houses with sunshine gushing out the skies as the romantic palm trees stood paralyzed near the seashore. And if you were magnificent at mumbling, picking your nose, getting lost and found in the bathroom, or losing your soul during some English exam, these credentials made you the class genius or clown.

Being left-handed didn't help either. I was often forced to write with my right hand. But it didn't work. I would not allow the stuffed shirts or The System to play football with my mind. I may have been "slow" with my ABCs at first, but I was definitely not some Juan Bobo or simpleton. No one was going to belittle me. My pride was intolerable!

I simply refused to give up my romantic accent. I was not going to be deprived of my freedom of self. While many fought back by joining street gangs like the Purple Knights or Young Sinners with switchblade tempers flashing out of their back-pockets, I was reading the dictionary like bible study. And what happened when I asked a classmate in Spanish what "homework" meant? My home-teacher, Mrs. Schaefer, with whom I first experienced puppy-love, held my hand down as she scratched it with her outrageous fingernails. I was sent to the dean, a mild-mannered hypocrite who rolled his newspaper tightly and with his reliable night-stick on my head, he screamed "Speak English only! Spanish is bad for you! Repeat: Speak English only! Spanish is bad for you!"

I was emotionally raped and left stranded in some corner of the world with a dunce cap on my head, and later forced to remain after school to write on three huge blackboards: Speak English. Spanish Is Bad For Me. I came home with a bilingual headache.

The next morning, Mama was dragged into the dean's office with my teacher and school principal pouring nasty syllables out of their mouths. They lashed out and killed me with their eyebrows.

Mama was confused and ashamed, as if I had set the school on fire. When I tried to explain myself to her, she slapped me hard across my face. I died crying inside. When I was ordered to return to class, the smirk on the faces of my classmates disheartened me. I drowned in my silence. And I could still remember Mama's slap across my face as if this happened yesterday.

I realized by then that the New York City Department of Education had declared war on my cultural heritage. But I was no longer resentful of the English language. I saw it as a deliberate conspiracy to make us fear *In-glish*, and succumb to invisibility. I chose to befriend English instead but kept my Spanish close to the heart. Still, it was a damn pity that we could not be accepted for having the best of two worlds, two great languages and cultures. I was determined to survive the American Dream machine with its melting pot recipe to conform while you turned your back on your own identity as you faded into cultural amnesia.

It taught me to be on guard. I developed crap-detecting antennas that gave me greater resilience when someone shook your hand while stabbing you in the back at the same time. I purposely chose not to return the hatred and racism so easily spit upon me. I recognized how education became warfare with its grading and tracking system. It degraded and undermined me.

When I became a high school teenager, though still off-the-wall with my second-hand clothes, leftover rice & bean sandwiches and awkward rock & roll rhythms, I escaped to the public libraries.

There I met the master poets and writers. such as Blake, Hemingway, Elisabeth Browning, Mark Twain, Emily Dickinson, Longfellow, Dostoyevsky, Langston Hughes, Steinbeck, Ginsberg, Amiri Baraka and Willie Shake. I secretly met these great voices from eye-to-mind and took them home to meet my Latino heartbeats: Cervantes, Dario, Lorca, Neruda, Martí, Luis Palés Matos, Piri Thomas, Llorens Torres and Julia de Burgos!

I read, observed, and absorbed. Reading and writing became my second skin, an embodiment of words given life to create fresh wind. The poet from within had emerged and evolved. Poetics became my calling, my confidant. Poetry was my badge of honor. My weapon! The quest was not to determine what poetry *Is*, but what it *Could Be*: A voice among many. I continued to search for my own roots while living the anonymous hope of a poet who believed that America will some day embrace me as part of its own national soul.

During these transformational years, I discovered that books written about Latinos were mostly loony tune caricatures of some Anglos' distorted vision of Boricuas and other *colorful* people. I was determined to create a spiritual and artistic balance in the present while getting a firm foot-hold on my future. I knew it was vital to define myself and not allow others to label me with negative stereotypes such as *minority*. Ironically, I am now a "hot" majority minority while millions of undocumented Latinos are written off as illegal aliens of the new and improved social underclass.

Unfortunately, the growing contributions made by Latinos across the oceans – in education, commerce, government, grassroots advocacy for health and human services, or in mass media, film, sports and arts entertainment was oftentimes left ignored - unless some misguided soul with a black or brown face was criminalized or lynched in the headlines.

Latinos are still depicted as migrant or immigrant sponges and rejects from the belly of the beast; particularly by right-wing political maggots and false religious prophets who blame the downfall of the federal budget on women, the elderly and misbegotten children who need this kind of tongue-lashing like they need domestic violence, HIV Aids, child abuse, or other societal ills less important than global warming or war-mongering by the birthers.

Yet, our Latino ancestry reflect incredible strength and veracity as one in our unanimity of being. We did not cross the border; it crossed us.

We will not disappear, then and now. We have been both part (and apart) of the American impulse and browning of this great nation way before it became America in 1776; and afterwards when it invaded Borinquen and turned its bootstraps into a perfumed colony (1952) with its embellished Manifest Destiny in the name of prosperity, democracy and food-stamp colonialism.

Like other newcomers before us, we played a major role in its continual redefinition, energy and emerging talent. The nagging issue of English-Only will not defeat Latinos who strongly believe in Spanish-Plus. America must understand that democratic principles do not solely exist in the English language, and that our universal heritage is undeniably inseparable from its own petrified roots.

Above all, Latinos are more than bilingual voices. They are just as multicultural as they are multinational. The word *minority* is a caste system with a cast call without an audition: When by nature the blend is greater than the ingredients alone. And perhaps for these and a millennium more reasons, I chose a gateway to advocate for the freedom to learn while Puerto Ricanizing America.

ACKNOWLEDGMENTS

Every word a poet writes on a page is a genesis with an uncharted journey before it emerges in a book with a life of its own. I came from a pearl of the Caribbean where reflection is a gift. Along the way, *Mama* led me to an enchanted forest of books where I was captivated like some vagabond desperado howling at the mysteries of silence as I learned to play and dance with words. Every poem was a new migration with a luggage full of indelible dreams. It was home where the poet became a rebel with a story to be told. I honor my mother Milagros whose quiet wisdom cultivated my passion for reading between the lines. Her love, determination and patriotic fervor nourished my imagination.

A Mirror In My Own Backstage grew its wings with the love and encouragement of *mi compañera,* Iris. Her guidance, steadfast vision, and editorial gifts paved every step of the way. It's been a transformative journey.

My thanks to Adrien Bibiloni Morales, who with media technology savvy at his fingerprints, sent my cantos into cyberspace with his youthful constellations.

I thank acclaimed artist Juan Sanchez who enthusiastically committed to create the cover art and design. His ancestral blend of the Arawak-Taíno and African tapestry of our rich Puerto Rican heritage, combining painting, photography and collage, is a work of art.

I am indebted to painter, illustrator and graphic artist Walter Velez for his original cover font and logo design for Red Sugarcane Press. He has motivated me to have a deeper appreciation for the craft of writing.

I express my gratitude to renowned scholar Edna Acosta-Belén for her reflections of my writings. Her trailblazing research as a leading voice of literary criticism about Puerto Rican, Hispanic Caribbean, and Latin American literature and gender studies in the United States has illuminated our social and political history like a sacred code of honor for Latinos across the globe.

To Richard Poe, I extend special thanks for his gifted mastery as a storyteller in writing the Foreword. A rare poet with a strong commitment to the integrity of a writer's vision, he once stopped cold and changed directions to master the art of terror with his own *Perfect Fears*. Poe has taught many writers to stand against the winds and to defend their creative freedom.

Newark poet laureate Amiri Baraka, the original Beat jazz hipster and prophetic provocateur, has been an incredible mentor. The legendary Baraka is always on the scene, forward thinking, hip on hypocrisy, still stepping on toes with a new kind of riff, faithful to the grammar of revolution for social justice.

I am thankful for the support of Magdalena Gómez whose pioneering work as a poet, performance artist, playwright, and educator has opened new passageways for creative expression to advance social causes. Gómez is a relentless warrior who fights so that the truth should never be whispered. I am also grateful to Tato Laviera for his support and poetic wisdom. Laviera is a *neo-criollo declamador* who captures the heartbeat of Puerto Rican and African Caribbean traditions. These brilliant versifiers enrich our cultural legacy.

I also thank my friend, photographer George Malave for his caring and creative insights. Our conversations about the clarity of thought in imagery and metaphor have been an inspiration deepened with humility.

Lastly but not least, I acknowledge the support of my holistic family at Boricua College, especially to president Dr. Victor G. Alicea and to my colleague Dr. Myrna Nieves for her persistent commitment to breaking ground/*abriendo caminos* for so many poets and writers.

No poet could ask for greater faith, clarity and purpose from such a loving family and lifelong friends.

José Angel Figueroa
Harlem, New York

ABOUT THE AUTHOR

José Angel Figueroa is a poet, playwright, actor, and professor of Puerto Rican, Latin American and Caribbean Literature. He is best known for his poetry -- a diverse body of work that reflects searing social commentary about cultural, gender, economic and political issues related to the Latino/a experience in the United States, Puerto Rico, and Latin America. One of the poets associated with the early years of the Neorican literary movement and the Nuyorican Poets Café, Figueroa has been credited as a major contributor to the Puerto Rican and Latino literary experience in *The Norton Anthology of Latino Literature, Harvest of Empire: A History of Latinos in America*, and *Harvard Educational Review*. He was one of the first New York poets to introduce his writings in Spanish to readers in Puerto Rico. His books include *Hypocrisy Held Hostage, Noo Jork,* and *East 110th Street,* and his writings have been published in numerous anthologies and literary journals.

Figueroa is also known for his work in the theater. He produced, wrote, and directed *A Tribute to the Life and Times and Work of Piri Thomas,* a multi-arts presentation. His play *Transnightification* was directed by Raul Julia at the Joseph Papp Public Theater and his jazz opera, *King of the Crabs,* was performed at Intar Hispanic American Theater. He also produced and directed *The Grassroots Poets Series* at Miriam Colon's Puerto Rican Traveling Theater.

Figueroa has taught and worked with students of all ages in public schools, colleges and universities, community venues and prisons. His work as a children's literature specialist and language arts consultant with public schools resulted in the editing and publishing of more than 66 volumes of original children's and youth writings.

Presently, Figueroa is a professor at Boricua College in New York City.

ABOUT THE ARTIST

Juan Sánchez is a visual artist living and working in Brooklyn, New York. He earned an MFA degree from the Mason Gross School of the Arts at Rutgers University in 1980 and a BFA from the Cooper Union School of Art in 1977. Sánchez has received several awards and fellowships such as the John Simon Guggenheim Memorial Foundation, the National Endowment for the Arts, New York Foundation for the Arts, The Joan Mitchell Foundation, and a Lifetime Achievement Award from the National Hispanic Academy of Media Arts and Sciences.

Sanchez' mixed media paintings, prints, photography and video work are exhibited nationally and internationally and are in the permanent collections of The Metropolitan Museum of Art, The Whitney Museum of American Art, The Museum of Modern Art, El Museo del Barrio, El Instituto de Cultura Puertoriquena in San Juan, Puerto Rico and Centro Wilfredo Lam in Havana, Cuba. He is a Professor and Deputy Chair of Studio Art at Hunter College, the City University of New York.

ABOUT RED SUGARCANE PRESS

The mission of Red Sugarcane Press is to present well-known and emerging artists and activists who reflect unique voices from the grassroots of the Puerto Rican, Caribbean, Latin@ and African diasporas. We seek to provide works that break new ground, provoke and challenge us to embrace new directions.

These works provide a deeper knowledge of our history that aim to educate and entertain. They also seek to inspire dialogue and to connect readers who love literature and social justice in the spirit of human liberation.

Red Sugarcane Press is rooted in the journey of indigenous and African peoples in the Americas who from the time of enslavement to the present have struggled for human rights and triumphed through the courage and tenacity of many generations.

www.redsugarcanepress.com

www.ingramcontent.com/pod-product-compliance
Lightning Source LLC
Chambersburg PA
CBHW051439290426
44109CB00016B/1620